BUILDING STRONG FAMILIES

FOUNDATIONS FOR THE FAMILY SERIES

BUILDING STRONG FAMILIES

DENNIS RAINEY,

EDITOR

CROSSWAY BOOKS

A DIVISION OF
GOOD NEWS PUBLISHERS
WHEATON, ILLINOIS

Building Strong Families

Copyright © 2002 by Dennis Rainey

Published by Crossway Books
    A division of Good News Publishers
    1300 Crescent Street
    Wheaton, Illinois 60187

Crossway's publication of *Building Strong Families* is in cooperation with FamilyLife and the Council on Biblical Manhood and Womanhood.

Cover design: David LaPlaca

Cover photo: PhotoDisc

First printing 2002

Printed in the United States of America

Scripture references marked NIV are from the Holy Bible: New International Version.® Copyright © 1973, 1978, 1984 by International Bible Society. Used by permission of Zondervan Publishing House. All rights reserved.

The "NIV" and "New International Version" trademarks are registered in the United States Patent and Trademark Office by International Bible Society. Use of either trademark requires the permission of International Bible Society.

Scripture references marked RSV are from the Revised Standard Version. Copyright © 1946, 1952, 1971, 1973 by the Division of Christian Education of the National Council of the Churches of Christ in the U.S.A.

Scripture references marked NASB are from the New American Standard Bible® Copyright © The Lockman Foundation 1960, 1962, 1963, 1968, 1971, 1972, 1973, 1975, 1977, 1995. Used by permission.

Scripture quotations marked ESV are from The Holy Bible, English Standard Version, copyright © 2001 by Crossway Bibles, a division of Good News Publishers. Used by permission. All rights reserved.

Scripture references marked KJV are from the King James Version of the Bible.

Library of Congress Cataloging-in-Publication Data
Building strong families / Dennis Rainey, editor.
    p.   cm. — (Foundations for the family series)
    Includes bibliographical references and index.
    ISBN 1-58134-382-5 (pbk. : alk. paper)
    1. Family—Religious aspects—Christianity—Congresses. 2. Family—
Religious life—Congresses. I. Rainey, Dennis, 1948–   . II. Series.
BT707.7 .B85 2002
248.8'45—dc21   2002000169
                                           CIP

15	14	13	12	11	10	09	08	07	06	05	04	03	02
15	14	13	12	11	10	9	8	7	6	5	4	3	2	1

CONTENTS

THE CONTRIBUTORS

Harold D. Davis is founder and Executive director of TALKS Mentoring of Champaign (Illinois), Inc. He is an ordained minister and is recognized as an Associate Minister at Canaan Missionary Baptist Church of Urbana, Illinois, where he sereved for twelve years as Assistant Pastor and Pastor of Youth Activities. Davis holds the Master of Ministry and Doctor of Ministry degrees with honors from Bethany Theological Seminary. He has authored several books, including *Never Alone (Dating from the Biblical Perspective)* and the TALKS Mentoring curriculum series. He has shared the ministry of TALKS Mentoring on "Focus on the Family," "Money Matters," and "FamilyLife Today." Davis has served on several boards of directors, including Youth for Christ and Boy Scouts of America. He is a frequent speaker for campus InterVarsity meetings and conducts retreats and seminars for men, youth, and singles, and along with his wife, Ollie Watts Davis, for married couples. The Davises have four children and reside in Champaign.

Steve Farrar is founder and Chairman of Men's Leadership Ministries. He is a graduate of California State University, Fullerton, holds a Master's degree from Western Seminary in Portland, Oregon, and has an earned doctorate from Dallas Theological Seminary. Farrar is the author of *Point Man: How a Man Can Lead His Family; Standing Tall; Finishing Strong;* and *Anchor Man*. His latest book is *Gettin' There: How a Man Finds His Way on the Trail of Life*. Farrar is a frequent speaker for Men's Leadership Ministries' conferences, Promise Keepers, and other events throughout the nation. Steve's wife, Mary, is completing her Master's degree at Dallas Theological Seminary. The Farrars have three children and reside in Dallas.

Wayne Grudem is Research Professor of Bible and Theology at Phoenix Seminary in Scottsdale, Arizona. Prior to Phoenix Seminary, he taught for twenty years at Trinity Evangelical Divinity School, Deerfield, Illinois, where he was chairman of the Department of Biblical and Systematic Theology. He received a B.A. from Harvard University, an M.Div. from Westminster Seminary, Philadelphia, and a Ph.D. (in New Testament) from the University of Cambridge, England. He has published eight books, including *Systematic Theology: An Introduction to Biblical Doctrine* and *Recovering Biblical Manhood and Womanhood* (coedited with John Piper). He is a cofounder and past president of the Council on Biblical Manhood and Womanhood, a past president of the Evangelical Theological Society, and a member of the Translation Oversight Committee for the English Standard Version of the Bible. He and his wife Margaret have been married since 1969 and have three adult sons.

Susan Hunt is the Women in the Church Consultant for the Christian Education and Publications Committee of the Presbyterian Church in America. She received her Bachelor of Christian Education from Columbia Theological Seminary. She has authored several books including *The True Woman*; *Heirs of the Covenant*; *By Design: God's Distinctive Calling for Women*; *Spiritual Mothering: The Titus 2 Mandate for Women Mentoring Women*; *Your Home—A Place of Grace*; and two children's books, including *My ABC Bible Verses*. She and her husband, Gene, a pastor, live in Marietta, Georgia. They have three adult children and nine grandchildren.

Bob Lepine is cohost of the nationally syndicated radio program, "FamilyLife Today." He speaks internationally on subjects related to marriage and family. He and his wife, Mary Ann, were married in 1979 and have five children. They live in Little Rock, Arkansas.

Robert Lewis is Teaching Pastor of Fellowship Bible Church in Little Rock, Arkansas. He has a Master of Divinity degree and a Master's degree in New Testament from Western Seminary in Portland, Oregon. He also earned a Doctorate of Ministry degree at

Talbot Seminary. He is the author of *Rocking the Roles* (with Bill Hendricks); *Real Family Values; Managing Pressures in Your Marriage* (with Dennis Rainey); *One to One; Raising a Modern Day Knight;* and most recently, *The Church of Irresistible Influence.* Lewis is a member of the governing council of the Council of Biblical Manhood and Womanhood and serves on the board of Leadership Network. He has also served on the speaker team for FamilyLife for eleven years. In 2001, he was chosen for the Hall of Honor by the National Coalition of Men's Ministries and was named "Pastor of the Year" by that organization. He and his wife, Sherard, have four children.

Crawford W. Loritts, Jr., is an associate director for Campus Crusade for Christ, USA. He has a Doctor of Sacred Theology degree from Philadelphia Biblical University, a Doctor of Divinity degree from Biola University, and a Doctor of Letters degree from Trinity International University. He is the author of four books: *A Passionate Commitment; Never Walk Away; Make It Home Before Dark;* and *Lessons from a Life Coach.* Loritts speaks for Promise Keeper events and other conferences and is the host of a daily radio program, "Living a Legacy." He and his wife, Karen, have been married for more than thirty years and have four adult children and one grandson. They make their home in the Atlanta area.

C. J. Mahaney is Senior Pastor of Covenant Life Church in the northern suburbs of Washington, D.C. He also leads PDI Ministries, which is involved in planting and supporting local churches in the United States, Mexico, Canada, and the United Kingdom. Mahaney serves on the board of the Christian Counseling and Educational Foundation (CCEF) and on the advisory council of the Council on Biblical Manhood and Womanhood (CBMW). Mahaney and his wife, Carolyn, have three daughters, one son, and one grandson. The Mahaneys live in Gaithersburg, Maryland.

John Piper has been Senior Pastor of Bethlehem Baptist Church in Minneapolis since 1980. Prior to that he taught Biblical Studies at Bethel College in St. Paul for six years. Piper holds degrees from Wheaton College (B.A.), Fuller Seminary (B.D.), and the University of Munich (D.Theol.). He has published many books, including

Desiring God: Meditations of a Christian Hedonist; The Pleasures of God; Recovering Biblical Manhood and Womanhood (coeditor); *A Hunger for God: Desiring God Through Fasting and Prayer; The Innkeeper;* and *Seeing and Savoring Jesus Christ.* Piper and his wife, Noël, live in Minneapolis and have four sons, a daughter, and two grandchildren.

Dennis Rainey is cofounder and Executive Director of FamilyLife and has published many books, including *Moments Together for Couples; Starting Your Marriage Right; One Home at a Time; Parenting Today's Adolescent; Preparing for Marriage; The New Building Your Mate's Self Esteem; The Tribute and the Promise; Ministering to Twenty-First Century Families;* and *We Still Do.* He is Senior Editor of the popular HomeBuilders couples series. A graduate of Dallas Theological Seminary, Rainey is the cohost of the award-winning nationally syndicated "FamilyLife Today" radio program. He and his wife, Barbara, are the parents of six children and have two grandchildren. They live near Little Rock, Arkansas.

Stu Weber is pastor of Good Shepherd Community Church near Gresham, Oregon. He is the father of three sons and an international speaker and author of the popular *Tender Warrior; Four Pillars of a Man's Heart; All the King's Men; Along the Road to Manhood;* and *Spirit Warriors.* A former Green Beret, Weber was awarded three Bronze Stars in Vietnam and today enjoys an active ministry to the U.S. military community.

INTRODUCTION

Dennis Rainey

———————

In March 2000, with jet aircraft rumbling above a DFW airport hotel, a strategic conference on the family created some noise of its own concerning the current condition and future of the Christian family.

At a historic meeting of church leaders assembled from across the United States, the "Building Strong Families in Your Church" conference aired and discussed virtually every key topic related to the family in the new millennium.

Cosponsored by FamilyLife and the Council on Biblical Manhood and Womanhood (CBMW), an impressive roster of speakers and seminar leaders probed topics as diverse as "How Submission Works in Practice," "Raising Modern-Day Knights and Ladies-in-Waiting," "Sexual Perversion," "Church Discipline," Putting the Internet to Work for the Family," and "Father Hunger Among a Lost Generation."

The result was a stimulating brew of the best of current thinking and practice related to family ministry in the church today. I am grateful that Crossway Books had the vision to help us capture many of these thoughtful presentations in written form.

A collection of four books entitled the Foundations for the Family Series ultimately will be released by Crossway. I am honored to join Nancy Leigh DeMoss and Wayne Grudem as editors of these volumes.

In this book crucial topics like the following are tackled with insight and spirit: how to raise masculine sons and feminine daughters; what local church family ministry should try to accomplish in the new millennium; mentoring of boys and young women; a vision for clear-eyed leadership; renewal of the home; the true roles of husbands and wives; sexual intimacy.

In addition to offering thanks to Nancy DeMoss and Wayne Grudem for their role in the conference as well as in this series, I would like to acknowledge my appreciation and gratitude for the work of my buddy and fellow warrior of words, Bruce Nygren, on this project. You're a good friend. A special thanks goes to Janet Logan, John Majors, Cherry Tolleson, Randy Likens, and Clark Hollingsworth for holding down the fort while I speak and write. You all are terrific.

As John Piper describes so eloquently later in this book, the surpassing goal for all we do is the "glory of God." I trust that the material presented herein, with God's assistance, will meaningfully accomplish that objective in your life and ministry.

I

OVERVIEW

1

Local Church Family Ministry in the New Millennium

Dennis Rainey

—∞∞∞—

No church, community, or nation will rise higher than the spiritual condition of its families.

Today our nation suffers from a sickness of the soul because our families are weak. Weak in their knowledge of God. Weak in their convictions about God. Weak in their experience of God. Weak in their understanding of how to love one another.

This is not how God intended it. The family is God's smallest unit in the battle for the soul of any nation. He designed the family as the birthplace and residence of Christianity. It is the place where the knowledge, fear, and love of the Lord are taught by parents and learned by children. The family is where character is planted and grown. It is the place where civility and respect for others are nurtured and cultivated.

If the soul of America is to be restored, it will be done one home, one family at a time, and in the church we assist that by proclaiming God's truth for the family. We need a "family reformation." Just as the Protestant Reformation restored vibrant faith to the soul, so a family reformation can restore spiritual vitality in our homes, communities, and nation.

With the prophet Jeremiah we cry out for America, "O land, land, land, hear the word of the LORD!" (Jer. 22:29, NASB).

ASSUMPTIONS OF A FAMILY REFORMATION

The local church plays a vital role in reforming the family, but before I present several mandates concerning the family for the church in the new millennium, I need to explain three critical assumptions that must be understood and embraced before we take action.

First, if we want to reform the family we need standards. If there is no measuring mechanism, no "spiritual yardstick," how will we evaluate progress?

The problem we face today was described perfectly many centuries ago by Jeremiah: "An appalling and horrible thing has happened in the land: the prophets prophesy falsely, and the priests rule on their own authority; and My people love it so! But what will you do at the end of it?" (Jer. 5:30-31, NASB). We live in a day of hyper-individualism, where rules are made to be broken—if they are made at all. The Bible is a book of grace but not of a lawless grace that says, "I'll do it my way, thank you." Augustine said, "When regard for the truth has broken down, all things become doubtful." We live in such a time.

When Scripture is not taught faithfully but is replaced by ungodly opinions and twisted interpretations, the end will be devastating. A picture of this appears in Isaiah 59, where truth is described as having "stumbled in the street" (v. 14, NASB). As a result moral decay overwhelmed God's people. Without the strength and stability of truth, those who did try to do right actually became evil's prey (v. 15). If we do not humble ourselves and live and breathe God's truth and righteousness, evil stands at the door, eager to devour us and our descendants.

This issue of convictions is so important because the enemy of our soul doesn't want parents to take a stand on anything. For example, consider the negative cultural values presented to our children through movies, advertising, fashion, television shows, books, the Internet, and dating customs. Parents who have convictions are rare.

Confusion reigns. As a result, boundaries for today's youth are unclear or nonexistent.

A family reformation will occur at the intersection where daily issues of life like these collide with God's unchanging truth. And where do most such "collisions" occur? *They occur at home, in every marriage and family.* That's where convictions must be clear.

Second, a family reformation will require courage. God said to Joshua (not once but three times) as he assumed leadership of the Israelites, "Be strong and courageous" (Josh. 1:6, 9, 18).

Our lack of courage today is partially a result of our having few convictions. Chuck Colson has said, "Courage does not follow rutted pathways." If we want to win a popularity contest in our families, churches, and ministries, we need only to follow the crowd down the road most traveled—the avenue of compromise. But if we want to proclaim the truth of God's Book, we will have to take the narrow path, where traffic is light.

Sometimes the courage required is not so much that of proclaiming God's Word in public but of living it out at home. It might be as basic as a husband seeking to pray regularly with his wife. A pastor I know once stood before a group of men and said, "I have been listening to the call to pray with my wife for ten years and haven't done it. But I am stepping forward today and doing the courageous thing. I will pray with my wife every day."

Or courage may be required of parents when their teenager says, "Mom, Dad, how far should I go with the opposite sex before I get married?" It seems that in the Christian community we don't know where to draw the line for our sons and daughters when it comes to premarital sex. We know we are against fornication and adultery, but our true convictions on activities that precede sexual intercourse are fuzzy. As a result, what happens to young people? They start down the slick slope of premarital intimacy and, without boundaries regarding sex, often slide over the edge. If clear, biblically based standards and boundaries concerning the opposite sex are absent, the world's standards will take their place. That's exactly what is happening to

Christian young people; they are accepting what the world preaches about marriage and family.

Barbara and I are doing our best to raise our children and keep them unstained by evil. In the area of relationships with the opposite sex, we have built a fence of behavior standards, not at the bottom of the slippery slope just before the cliff's edge, but far inland. For example, we have challenged our children to save their first kiss for their spouse at the wedding altar. Have all of them done that? No. But we will never know what personal devastation we have prevented by having the courage to hold up this high standard. (I know you may not agree with our challenge to our sons and daughters, and I have no problem with that. But I do want to ask you, what are your standards and boundaries? Where will you draw the line with your children concerning physical involvement with the opposite sex?)

Third, a family reformation will require innovative strategies and new tactics by local churches. If we are going to see positive, enduring change in families, we will have to abandon some old practices and embrace some new ones. Our God is creative and dynamic. He gives us the freedom to slay sacred cows. We can retire programs that are obsolete. Times have changed. The culture has spent and squandered moral and spiritual capital inherited from our forefathers. We must reinvest and rebuild. It's time to create new church infrastructures of ministry to the family. To do that, I propose four mandates for family ministry in the new millennium.

FOUR MANDATES FOR THE NEW MILLENNIUM CHURCH

Before I launch these ideas I want to express my admiration for the men and women who lead various ministries of the local church. I have been an elder and have many close friends who are pastors. I have helped shoulder their weight on many occasions and know this role is one of the more difficult assignments in all of life. I offer these mandates in the spirit of a servant, someone who eagerly desires a more spiritually healthy environment for ministry to families. My goal is not to add more weight to a load of responsibility that is already heavy. I sincerely think that these challenges to change local church ministry to the family will drastically improve effectiveness and bring needed spiritual renewal.

Mandate One: A Family Reformation Must Start in Your Home and Mine

In our ministry at FamilyLife we often spend time interviewing pastors. As we have probed to learn their most compelling needs related to family ministry, one issue has risen above all others: "My marriage and family."

I now am convinced that the number one reason many pastors do not preach more on the marriage covenant, come down hard on divorce, encourage prayer with spouse or children, or advocate family altars and devotions is that they see their own wives in the second pew and they know that such things are not happening in their own homes. So the topics are avoided, or are touched on only lightly. And the other families in the church then suffer and continue their slow slide.

Psalm 101 presents some guidelines for those of us who want to be effective leaders in ministry: "I will walk within my house in the integrity of my heart" (v. 2). Later the same Psalm advises, "He who walks in a blameless way is the one who will minister to me" (v. 6). In other words, if we want change in the families of those we lead, we have to lead and shepherd our own families. We will never do this perfectly, of course, but we must seek to walk in integrity at home. And if we make mistakes, we need to be quick to repent and ask forgiveness.

Is there anything you need to repent of on the home front? Selfishness? Passivity? Arrogance? Anger? Disrespect for the needs of your spouse? Ignoring your children? Anger at a child who is difficult to love? Are you attracted to someone other than your spouse? Are you playing with matches that could spark an emotional affair? If I experience temptation in this area, I tell Barbara, "I just need you to know what I'm thinking and what I've been tempted with."

Perhaps you are involved in an inappropriate dialogue on an Internet chat room or are being enticed by pornography. No matter what the sin, it is compromising your integrity at home. Repent, and get rid of it.

Advancing a family reformation may mean tackling any number of issues, such as resolving a lingering conflict with your spouse, or starting to read the Scriptures and pray with your children each night at bedtime. For a number of years I led Bible studies with business-men, but I gave that up for a decade because I could not go on lead-ing a Bible study with businessmen if I wasn't doing one with my own children before they left for school. Ask God to show you where the reformation needs to begin at your house.

Mandate Two: The Church Must Become a Marriage and Family Equipping Center

Equipping husbands and wives in marriage, as well as training parents to lead their children spiritually, are not "just another part" of local church ministry; they represent the greatest opportunity for the local church to spread the gospel, build spiritual maturity, and advance the Kingdom of God in this generation! The needs in the family dwarf all other personal felt needs in Western civilization. In America, as peo-ple wake up and begin their day, what other issue causes them as much anxiety and pain? What issue could compare in intensity and scope to needs related to marriage and family?

Some of the evidence to support this would be humorous if it were not so poignant. A case in point is a *New York Times* story which reported on a course led by a psychotherapist to train businesswomen how to find a man and get married. It's called "Marriage Works" and is referred to as a "finishing school for feminists." The six-month course includes 276 hours of instruction and costs $9,600! I wonder what *Ms.* magazine thinks of this. The women taking this course evi-dently have found that personal fulfillment through career, a high income, and the like are not the whole answer. They are willing to pay big dollars to learn how to make a relationship work.[1]

Widespread desires like these represent a huge opportunity for local churches. We have a generation coming of age that is screaming, "How do you do marriage and family?" They're coming from broken homes. Their parents' marriages didn't work. They are skeptical and afraid. And guess who could provide the answers? The local church!

Our God created the family. Ministry to families is not a strategy, a goal, or a program; ministry to families must permeate all the church does, because faith formation begins at home (Deut. 6:1-9). If we ignore this reality, the church's job is made much more difficult.

Meanwhile, where do we in the church stand on family issues? For the most part, we're playing defense. This is understandable, because we are overwhelmingly a culture influenced by divorce. My pastor, Robert Lewis, said once about our church's staff, which at the time numbered more than sixty-five, "The time our church staff spends either preventing divorce, helping people go through divorce, or helping people recover from a divorce, now encompasses more of our time than all other issues combined."

Now if I were the devil, I would want to get all the church staffs in America totally on the defensive, spending hours each week untangling relational mayhem. What would happen if we could reduce that commitment of staff resources in half? Just think what we could accomplish for the advancement of the gospel with all of that fresh energy!

So how might we bring changes here?

First, we need to become intentional about equipping marriages and families to be distinctively Christian. Ephesians 4:11 says that Christ gave pastors and teachers "for the equipping of the saints for the work of service, to the building up of the body of Christ" (Eph. 4:12, NASB). But where does the work of service start? Sunday school? The sermon? Wednesday night prayer meeting? No, it begins at home. We need to dust off a little saying from the fifties: "The family that prays together stays together." The culture is ripe for the church to step forward with spiritual initiatives that bring hope to families.

Second, we need to know the needs of our church families. You may be thinking, *Yeah, I counsel a lot. I know the needs of our people.* I'm sure that is true as far as it goes. But modern methods and technology allow even more sophisticated measurements of what people are thinking and what they need. For example, FamilyLife offers churches a resource called the Family Needs Survey.[2] We call it a "CT scan for a congregation." More than 27,000 church members nationwide have completed the research, and the aggregate findings are interesting: Of the top ten most-often-mentioned topics which respondents said they "currently need help with in their life," half of the issues related to marriage and parenting. These include "good communication," "children's spiritual growth," "spouse's needs/expectations," "building a strong marriage," and "Christian values in the home." Of those who are parents, 66 percent agreed with the statement, "I don't have much confidence in my parenting skills."

Now add in the present-day uncertainties and fears related to terrorist acts and we have a giant spiritual vacuum that needs to be filled in marriages and families across our nation. People have never been as spiritually receptive as they are today. They want answers that help them where they live at home with their spouse and families.

Do you sense the opportunity? People are hungry for what God says about the family issues they are facing. Let's find some fresh new ways to feed them a tasty meal.

Mandate Three: The Church Must Become the Guardian of the Marriage Covenant

Because marriage is a covenant among a man, a woman, and almighty God for a lifetime, no wonder God said that He hates divorce (Mal. 2:16). One reason God despises marital demise so much is that He desires godly offspring (Mal. 2:15). We are well aware of the personal, lifelong devastation experienced by many children of divorce. Novelist Pat Conroy has profoundly written that each divorce is the death of a small civilization. God hates this. It is not the model He intended.

Sometimes when I speak, I take a poll of the audience. I have found that only about one out of every three hundred in a Christian audience have ever seen a marriage covenant—not a marriage license, but a signed and witnessed covenant. By contrast, about one of four have seen a prenuptial agreement. What's wrong with that picture?

In our society we have "dumbed-down" the marriage promise so that in perceived seriousness it's about one notch above a car loan. In fact, I think in most states you probably can get out of marriage easier than you can ditch a car loan! It's time for the church to step forward and become the guardian, protector, and enforcer of the marriage covenant. It is time for the Christian community to say no to easy divorce and yes to a marriage covenant that lasts a lifetime. This is not time for religious business as usual. It is time for radical action.

How's this for an example of radical action taken by one pastor: He will not marry a couple if the bride-to-be intends to work outside the home after the wedding. This pastor says that he is "challenged most on this point before marriage. . . . but thanked most for it afterwards. The evidence is overwhelming in support of this position."[3] This requirement may seem "way out there," but this is not happening at some small church isolated from real life. This pastor is the former president of the Southern Baptist Convention, Tom Elliff, and his church near Oklahoma City has a membership of many thousands. Yes, Tom's approach is extreme compared to the positions of most churches these days. But do not disastrous circumstances call for seemingly radical solutions? People take shots at Tom for his stand, but are their methods producing better results?

Divorce is sweeping through the church in epidemic proportions today. Could it be that we need some radical treatment to reverse the trends? How will you address permanence in marriage in your church?

Upholding the marriage covenant begins with the care and nurture of your own covenant. Also, as your children grow up and marry, etch on their souls the sacredness of their marriage vows and covenant. Barbara and I did this when our daughter Ashley was engaged to Michael. We had their vows inscribed on fine paper by a calligrapher. Then during their wedding ceremony, the bride and bridegroom signed the document. To indicate our support of their marriage, Barbara and I signed the covenant too, as did many other family members and guests. The covenant was framed and now hangs in a prominent position in their home. Since then, two of our sons have married and both included such a marriage covenant document as a part of their wedding ceremony. I can't tell you how much meaning this has added to these weddings and to their marriages.

Finally, those in church leadership need to call others to fulfill their marriage covenant. Abraham Lincoln said, "To sin by silence when one should protest makes cowards of men." Let's not be empty-chested. Let's challenge people to honor their marriage vows. Let's protest vigorously when they seek to abandon them. Perhaps we should observe an annual "marriage covenant Sunday" in our churches. This could become a national statement by the Christian church on behalf of the permanence of marriage. What would happen if just ten thousand churches in America declared a Sunday every year to exalt the marriage covenant? Couples could face each other and renew their vows. Friends could sign a couple's marriage covenant document and by doing so say, "We will hold you accountable to keep your vows." I believe the divorce rate in evangelical churches would plummet.

A church in Georgia has had a marriage vow renewal ceremony annually since 1931. In those decades thousands have renewed their commitments to each other. Even couples that don't attend this church show up on this special Sunday to renew their marriage covenants.

The nation is desperate for the church to lead in protecting the institution of marriage. Let's just "do it."

Mandate Four: Challenge Lay People to Become
Marriage and Family Mentors

Dietrich Bonhoeffer wrote, "The righteous man is the one who lives for the next generation." Are we losing our generational vision, our responsibility to sow the seeds of truth and holiness that will bear fruit in our children and grandchildren? We need laymen and women to rediscover the vision of having God use them to reach back to a younger generation and lead them on to maturity. This won't just happen. Such mentors will need to be recruited to such a vision and mission.

Harold Davis is one of my heroes. He leads a small ministry that recruits Christian men to mentor African-American boys. As Harold explained, "When the older generation of men does not step down and pull the younger generation up, that [next] generation perishes." I fear this is happening today.

One way to build a mentor corps is to set a three-year goal to recruit five mentor couples for every one hundred people in a local church. Mentors need to be made available first to couples in the first five years of their marriage. Statistically, that is when the divorce rate is at its peak. Of the five couples per hundred, I would assign one to pre-marrieds and a second to newly married couples. Then I would find two couples who are parenting mentors, one for young children (preschool through elementary) and one for parents of adolescents. You also need crisis mentors, a couple whose marriage was rescued from trouble, who can come with encouragement to help other couples whose marriages are in trouble.

If you establish these mentor couples and present them to your church some Sunday, members of your congregation will respond enthusiastically to this mentoring initiative. The problem is not finding the people who want to be mentored, but challenging the right people to be mentors. Leaders in the local church and in parachurch ministry need to call on laymen to step out of their comfort zone, to step out of the bleachers, and to step onto the battlefield to win the war for the soul of the family.

Those are my mandates for furthering a family reformation. The task is substantial and may require more than a generation to complete, if the Lord tarries. But I believe it is a battle our generation must fight.

The importance and value of the cause is demonstrated over and over. Here's just one story. In 1999 FamilyLife began holding a large arena event called I Still Do. To date, nearly 200,000 men and women have gathered for a day to honor the marriage covenant and to focus on how to do a family "right." In the fall of 2000 I received some interesting letters from a woman I will call Melanie (some details have been altered to maintain confidentiality). With permission I share this family's inspiring story:

> Melanie and her husband, Larry, started dating when she was just sixteen. They married seven years later and eventually had three

children. From the outside, Melanie and Larry's marriage looked great. They attended a strong evangelical church in a major city and regularly "tuned up" their relationship at marriage conferences. They sought to have a positive influence on other couples and were often described in their circles as the "perfect little family" having the "perfect marriage." But life was not as perfect as it appeared.

Melanie had suspicions about Larry's faithfulness and hired a private detective. To her horror she found out that her husband in fact was having an affair with a woman he had met through his business.

Melanie was crushed, but providentially three days before receiving the sad news, she found a note on her car that read:

Dear Sister in Christ, Jesus loves you. Praise God for all things, Jeremiah 29:11—"For I know the plans I have for you, declares the Lord, plans to prosper you and not to harm you, plans to give you hope and a future. Then you will call upon me and come and pray to me, and I will listen to you. You will seek me and find me when you seek me with all you heart."

Melanie clung to that promise from God through her pain and suffering in the following days—during and after her initial confrontation with Larry.

As the weeks passed Melanie's anger turned to sadness as in reality she mourned the loss of someone she loved. But the anger returned abruptly one night when a discussion with Larry turned into an argument. The two were exchanging verbal blows in their family room where on the wall, surrounded by family photos, hung their nicely-framed marriage covenant. In a special ceremony Melanie and Larry had signed the covenant with their three children as witnesses. The kids fully understood what the words of the covenant meant, because their parents had reassured them frequently that "Mommy and Daddy loved each other and would never ever get divorced."

During their argument Melanie kept glancing at the marriage covenant. Understandably, the sight of it made her angry. She thought, *He lied to me . . . he promised me that he would always love me. . . . he promised he would be faithful.* Finally reaching her boiling point, Melanie jumped up, yanked the covenant off the wall, slammed it on the floor, and screamed: "This means nothing to you! Why did you sign it?" The glass in the frame shattered in a thousand pieces. Melanie picked up the paper covenant and crumpled it.

While this scene unfolded, the children, who had been banished to an upstairs room, heard the tinkling glass and wanted to come downstairs. They were curious about what had happened, but Larry yelled at them to stay away. A sobbing Melanie and her sobered husband swept up the glass and threw the broken frame and covenant in a garbage can.

After this storm, the couple went in another room and continued their discussion in a more civilized manner.

Meanwhile the kids continued to beg. Melanie and Larry relented and the children saw immediately the large blank spot on the wall. Their nine-year-old son John, in particular, was upset and kept coming to his parents telling them how bare the wall looked and that something must be done about it. Melanie and Larry reassured him that they would find something to hang on the wall.

A while later John returned and began bugging his mom and dad, saying he needed to show them something. They ignored him for a few minutes, but finally John dragged them into the family room. He pointed to the wall and said, "There, I fixed it!"

Larry and Melanie looked at each other and broke into tears. On the wall hung their battered covenant. John had rescued the crumpled paper from the trashcan, smoothed it out, wedged it into the frame, and hung it back on the wall. This boy desperately wanted to fix his parents' marriage and believed re-hanging their covenant was a good way to start the process. The covenant is still on that wall today—no glass and wrinkled—but it hangs.

And John's moving intervention did help spur Larry and Melanie into a process of reconciliation. . . .

Melanie wrote, "Isn't it awesome how God used this situation to break his [Larry's] heart and move him towards repentance."[4]

Yes, it is awesome what God can and will do to keep a family together. He longs to turn millions of weak families into bastions of strength. Will we join Him in saving homes in the new millennium?

NOTES

1. Abby Ellin, "Personal Business: A Class Feminists Might Abhor," *New York Times,* March 5, 2000.
2. For information, call 1-800-404-5052. Each church receives a detailed report of needs by demographic groups within the congregation. The spiritual condition of marriages and families is measured.
3. Tom Elliff, quoted in Dennis Rainey, *Ministering to Twenty-First Century Families* (Nashville: Word, 2001), 102.
4. This story originally appeared in Dennis Rainey and Barbara Rainey, gen. eds., *We Still Do* (Nashville: Thomas Nelson, 2001), 3. Used by permission.

2

THE KEY ISSUES IN THE MANHOOD-WOMANHOOD CONTROVERSY

Wayne Grudem

―⌘―

Very early in the Bible we read that both men and women are made "in the image of God." In fact, the very first verse that tells us that God created human beings also tells us that both "male and female" are in the image of God: "So God created man in his own image, in the image of God he created him; male and female he created them" (Gen. 1:27).[1]

To be in the image of God is an amazing privilege. It means to be like God and to represent God.[2] No other creatures in all of creation, not even the powerful angels, are said to be in the image of God. It is a privilege given only to us as men and women. We are more like God than any other creatures in the universe, for we alone are "in the image of God."[3]

Any discussion of biblical manhood and womanhood must start here. Every time we look at each other or talk to each other as men and women, we should remember that the person we are talking to is *more like God than anything else in the universe,* and that men and women share that status equally. Therefore we should treat men and women with equal dignity, knowing that men and women have equal value. Nowhere does the Bible say that men are more in God's image than women.[4] Men and women share equally in the tremendous privilege of being in the image of God.

The Bible thus from the very beginning corrects the errors of male dominance and male superiority that have come as the result of sin and that have been seen in nearly all cultures in the history of the world. Wherever men are thought to be better than women, wherever husbands act as selfish dictators, wherever wives are forbidden to have their own jobs outside the home or to vote or to own property or to be educated, wherever there is abuse or violence against women, or rape or female infanticide or polygamy or harems, and wherever women are treated as inferior, the biblical truth of equality in the image of God is being denied. To all societies and cultures where such things occur, we must proclaim that the very first page of God's Word bears a fundamental and irrefutable witness against these evils.[5]

Yet we can say even more. If men and women are equally in the image of God, then they are equally important to God and equally valuable to Him. This truth should exclude all feelings of pride or inferiority, that one sex is better or worse than the other. In contrast to the views of many non-Christian cultures and religions, no one should feel proud or superior because he is a man, and no one should feel disappointed or inferior because she is a woman. That God thinks men and women to be equal in value settles forever the question of personal worth, for God's evaluation is the true standard of personal value for all eternity.

Further evidence of our equality in the image of God is seen in the New Testament church, where the Holy Spirit is given in new fullness to both men and women (Acts 2:17-18), where both men and women are baptized into the body of Christ (Acts 2:41),[6] and where both men and women receive spiritual gifts for use in the life of the church (1 Cor. 12:7, 11; 1 Pet. 4:10). The apostle Paul reminds us that we are not to be divided into factions that think of themselves as superior and inferior (such as Jew and Greek, or slave and free, or male and female), but rather that we should think of ourselves as united beacuse we are all "one" in Christ Jesus (Gal. 3:28).

By way of application to marriage, this teaching on equality in the image of God is being neglected whenever husbands and wives do not listen respectfully and thoughtfully to each other's viewpoints, or do not value the wisdom that might be arrived at differently and expressed differently from the other person, or do not value the other person's different gifts and preferences as much as their own.

Speaking personally, I do not think I listened very well to my wife, Margaret, early in our marriage. I did not value her different gifts and preferences as much as my own, or her wisdom, which she arrived at and expressed differently. Later we made much progress in this area, but, looking back, Margaret told me that early in our marriage it felt as though her voice was taken away, and as though my ears were closed. I wonder if there are other couples in many churches where God needs to open the husband's ears to listen, and restore the wife's voice to speak.[7]

In July 1999, Campus Crusade for Christ issued its "Marriage and Family Statement." In part, it summarized a healthy perspective on the way equality manifests itself in marriage. After three paragraphs discussing both equality and differences between men and women, the statement says the following:

> In a marriage lived according to these truths, the love between husband and wife will show itself in listening to each other's viewpoints, valuing each other's gifts, wisdom, and desires, honoring one another in public and in private, and always seeking to bring benefit, not harm, to one another.[8]

Why do I list this as a key issue in the manhood-womanhood controversy? Not because we differ with egalitarians[9] on this question, but because we differ at this point with sinful tendencies in our own hearts, and with oppressive male chauvinism and male dominance. I also list it as a key issue because anyone preaching on manhood and womanhood has to start here—where the Bible starts—not with our differences but with our equality in the image of God.

Pastors wishing to teach on biblical manhood and womanhood in their churches must start here, affirming equality in the image of God, or they simply will not get a hearing. If they cannot start with male-female equality in the image of God, they may need to ask themselves if their hearts are right in dealing with this issue.

There is one more reason why I think this is a key issue, one that speaks especially to men. I think that one reason God has allowed this whole controversy on manhood and womanhood to enter the church at this time is so that we could correct some mistakes, change some wrongful traditions, and become more faithful to Scripture by treating our wives and all women with dignity and respect. The first step in correcting these mistakes is to be fully convinced in our hearts that women share equally with us men in the value and dignity that belongs to being made in the image of God.

KEY ISSUE 2: MEN AND WOMEN HAVE DIFFERENT ROLES IN MARRIAGE AS PART OF THE CREATED ORDER

When the members of the Council on Biblical Manhood and Womanhood wrote the "Danvers Statement" in 1987, we included the following affirmations:

> 1. Both Adam and Eve were created in God's image, equal before God as persons and distinct in their manhood and womanhood.
> 2. Distinctions in masculine and feminine roles are ordained by God as part of the created order, and should find an echo in every human heart.
> 3. Adam's headship in marriage was established by God before the Fall, and was not a result of sin.[10]

The statement adopted by the Southern Baptist Convention in June 1998 and affirmed (with one additional paragraph) by Campus Crusade in July 1999, also affirms God-given differences:

> The husband and wife are of equal worth before God, since both are created in God's image. The marriage relationship models the way God relates to His people. A husband is to love his wife as Christ

loved the church. He has the God-given responsibility to provide for, to protect, and to lead his family. A wife is to submit herself graciously to the servant leadership of her husband even as the church willingly submits to the headship of Christ. She, being in the image of God as is her husband and thus equal to him, has the God-given responsibility to respect her husband and to serve as his helper in managing the household and nurturing the next generation.[11]

By contrast, egalitarians do not affirm such created differences. In fact, the "Statement on Men, Women and Biblical Equality," published by Christians for Biblical Equality (CBE) says:

1. The Bible teaches that both man and woman were created in God's image, had a direct relationship with God, and shared jointly the responsibilities of bearing and rearing children and having dominion over the created order (Gen 1:26-28). . . .

5. The Bible teaches that the rulership of Adam over Eve resulted from the Fall and was therefore not a part of the original created order. . . .

10. The Bible defines the function of leadership as the empowerment of others for service rather than as the exercise of power over them (Matt 20:25-28, 23:8; Mark 10:42-45; John 13:13-17; Gal 5:13; 1 Peter 5:2-3). . . .

11. The Bible teaches that husbands and wives are heirs together of the grace of life and that they are bound together in a relationship of mutual submission and responsibility (1 Cor 7:3-5; Eph 5:21; 1 Peter 3:1-7; Gen 21:12). The husband's function as "head" (*kephale*) is to be understood as self-giving love and service within this relationship of mutual submission (Eph 5:21-33; Col 3:19; 1 Peter 3:7).[12]

So which position is right? Does the Bible really teach that men and woman had different roles from the beginning of creation?

When we look carefully at Scripture, I think we can see at least ten indications that God gave men and women distinct roles before the Fall, and particularly, that there was male headship in marriage before the Fall.

Ten Indications of Male Headship in Marriage Before the Fall

1. *The order.* Adam was created first, then Eve (note the sequence in Genesis 2:7 and 2:18-23). We may not think this is important today, but it was important to the biblical readers, and the apostle Paul sees it as important. He bases his argument for different roles in the assembled New Testament church on the fact that Adam was created prior to Eve. He says, "I permit no woman to teach or to have authority over men. . . . For Adam was formed first, then Eve . . ." (1 Tim. 2:12-13). According to Scripture itself, then, the fact that Adam was created first has implications not just for Adam and Eve themselves but also for the relationships between men and women generally throughout the church age.[13]

2. *The representation.* Adam, not Eve, had a special role in representing the human race. Looking at the Genesis narrative, we find that Eve sinned first, and then Adam sinned (Gen. 3:6: "she took of its fruit and ate; and she also gave some to her husband, and he ate"). Since Eve sinned first, we might expect the New Testament to say that we inherit a sinful nature because of Eve's sin, or that we are counted guilty because of Eve's sin. But this is not the case. In fact, it is just the opposite. We read in the New Testament, "For as *in Adam* all die, so also in Christ shall all be made alive" (1 Cor. 15:22). The New Testament does not say, "as in Eve all die . . ."

This is further seen in the parallel between Adam and Christ, where Paul views Christ as the "last Adam":

> Thus it is written, "The first man Adam became a living being"; the last Adam became a life-giving spirit. . . . The first man was from the earth, a man of dust; the second man is from heaven. . . . Just as we have borne the image of the man of dust, we shall also bear the image of the man of heaven (1 Cor. 15:45-49; see also Rom. 5:12-21, where another relationship between Adam and Christ is developed).

It is unmistakable, then, that Adam had a leadership role in representing the entire human race, a leadership role that Eve did not have. Nor was it true that Adam and Eve *together* represented the human race. It was Adam alone who represented the human race, because he had a particular leadership role that God had given him, a role that Eve did not share.

3. *The naming of woman.* When God made the first woman and "brought her to the man," the Bible says, "Then the man said, 'This at last is bone of my bones and flesh of my flesh; *she shall be called Woman,* because she was taken out of Man'" (Gen. 2:23). When Adam says, "she shall be called Woman," he is giving her a name. This is important because in the original context-readers would have understood that the person doing the "naming" of created things is the person who has authority over those things. In order to avoid the idea that Adam's naming of woman implies male leadership or authority, some egalitarians (such as Gilbert Bilezikian) deny that Adam gives a name to his wife in Genesis 2:23.[14] But his objection is hardly convincing when we see how Genesis 2:23 fits into the pattern of naming activities throughout these first two chapters of Genesis. We see this when we examine the places where the same verb (the Hebrew verb *qārā',* "to call") is used in contexts of naming in Genesis 1–2:

God *called* the light Day, and the darkness he called Night (1:5).

And God *called* the firmament Heaven (1:8).

God *called* the dry land Earth, and the waters that were gathered together he called Seas (1:10).

So out of the ground the Lord God formed every beast of the field and every bird of the air, and brought them to the man to see what he would *call* them; and whatever the man *called* every living creature, that was its name (2:19).

The man *gave names* to all cattle, and to the birds of the air, and to every beast of the field (2:20).

Then the man said, "This at last is bone of my bones and flesh of my flesh; she shall be *called* Woman, because she was taken out of Man" (2:23).

In each of these verses prior to Genesis 2:23, the same verb, the Hebrew verb *qārā'*, had been used. Just as God demonstrated His sovereignty over day and night, heavens, earth, and seas by assigning them names, so Adam demonstrated his authority over the animal kingdom by assigning them names. The pattern would have been easily recognized by the original readers, and they would have seen a continuation of the pattern when Adam said, "she shall be *called* Woman."

The original readers of the Old Testament would have been familiar with this pattern, a pattern whereby people who have authority over another person or thing have the ability to name that person or thing, a name that often indicates something of that person's character or quality. Thus, parents give names to their children (Gen. 4:25-26; 5:3, 29; 16:15; 19:37-38; 21:3). God even changes the names of people when He wishes to indicate a change in their character or role (Gen. 17:5, 15, where God changes Abram's name to Abraham and Sarai's name to Sarah). In each of these passages the same verb (*qārā'*) is used as in Genesis 2:23, and in each case the person who gives the name is one in authority over the person who receives the name. Therefore when Adam gives his wife the name "Woman," in terms of biblical patterns of thought this indicates a kind of authority that God gave to Adam, a leadership function that Eve did not have with respect to her husband.

We should notice here that Adam does not give the personal name "Eve" to his wife until Genesis 3:20 ("the man called [*qārā'*] his wife's name Eve, because she was the mother of all living"). This is because in the creation story in Genesis 2, Adam is giving a broad category name to his wife, indicating the name that would be given to womanhood generally, and He is not giving specific personal names designating the character of the individual.[15]

4. *The naming of the human race.* God named the human race "Man," not "Woman." Because the idea of "naming" is so important in the Old Testament, it is interesting what name God chose for the human race as a whole. We read, "When God created man, he made him in the likeness of God. Male and female he created them, and he blessed them *and named them Man* when they were created" (Gen. 5:1-2).

In the Hebrew text, the word translated "Man" is *'ādām*. This was by no means a gender-neutral term in the eyes of the Hebrew reader, because prior to Genesis 5:2 the Hebrew word *'ādām* has been used many times to speak of a male human being in distinction from a female human being. In the following list the word "man" represents this Hebrew word *'ādām* in every case:

> And the rib which the Lord God had taken from the man he made into a woman and brought her to the *man* (Gen. 2:22; we should notice here that it does not say that God made the rib into another *'ādām*, another "man," but that He made the rib into a woman, which is a different Hebrew word).
>
> The *man* said, "This at last is bone of my bone and flesh of my flesh; she shall be called Woman" (2:23).
>
> And the *man* and his wife were both naked and were not ashamed (2:25).
>
> And the *man* and his wife hid themselves from the presence of the Lord God (3:8).
>
> But the Lord God called to the *man,* and said to him, "Where are you?" (3:9).
>
> The *man* said, "The woman you put here with me—she gave me some fruit from the tree, and I ate it" (3:12, NIV).
>
> The *man* called his wife's name Eve (3:20).

When we come, then, to the naming of the human race in Genesis 5:2 (recounting an event that had occurred before the Fall), the original readers would have understood the clear male overtones or nuances. In fact, in the first four chapters of Genesis, the word *'ādām* had been used thirteen times to refer not to a human being in general but to a *male* human being. In addition to the eight examples mentioned above, it was used a further five times as a proper name for Adam in distinction from Eve (Gen. 3:17, 21; 4:1, 25; 5:1).[16]

We are not saying that the word *'ādām* in the Hebrew Bible always refers to a male human being, for sometimes it has a broader sense and means something like "person," but here in the early chapters of Genesis the connection with the man in distinction from the woman is a clear pattern. God gave the human race a name which, like the English word "man," can either mean a male human being or refer to the human race in general.

Does this make any difference? It does give a hint of male leadership, which God suggested in choosing this name. It is significant that God did not call the human race "Woman." (I am speaking, of course, of Hebrew equivalents to these English words.) Nor did He give the human race a name such as "humanity," which would have no male connotations and no connection with the man in distinction from the woman. Rather, He called the race "man." Raymond C. Ortlund rightly says, "God's naming of the race 'man' whispers male headship."[17] God "blessed them and named them Man *when they were created*" (Gen. 5:2).

If the name "man" in English (as in Hebrew) did not suggest male leadership or headship in the human race, there would be no objection to using the word "man" to refer to the human race generally today. But it is precisely the hint of male leadership in the word that has led some people to object to its use and to substitute other terms.[18] Yet it is that same hint of male leadership that makes this precisely the best translation of Genesis 1:27 and 5:2.

5. *The primary accountability.* After the Fall, God spoke to Adam first. In Genesis 3:9 we read, "But the Lord God called to the man, and said to him, 'Where are you?'" (Gen. 3:9). In the Hebrew text, the expression "the man" and the pronouns "him" and "you" are all singular. Even though Eve had sinned first, God first summoned Adam to give account for what had happened. This suggests that Adam was the one primarily accountable for what had happened in his family.

An analogy to this is seen in everyday family life. When a parent comes into a room where several children have been misbehaving, the parent will probably summon the oldest and say, "What happened here?" This is because, though all are responsible for their behavior, the oldest child bears the primary responsibility. In a similar way, when

God summoned Adam to give an account, it indicated a primary responsibility for Adam in the conduct of his family. This is similar to the situation in Genesis 2:15-17, where God had given commands to Adam alone before the Fall, indicating there also Adam's primary responsibility. By contrast, the serpent spoke to Eve first (Gen. 3:1), trying to get her to take responsibility for leading the family into sin, thus inverting the order that God had established at creation.

6. *The purpose.* Eve was created as a helper for Adam, not Adam as a helper for Eve. After God had created Adam and had given him directions concerning his life in the Garden of Eden, we read that the Lord God said, "It is not good that the man should be alone; I will make him a helper fit for him" (Gen. 2:18).

It is true that the Hebrew word here translated "helper" (*'ēzer*) is often used of God as our helper (e.g., Ps. 33:20; 70:5; 115:9). But the word "helper" does not by itself decide the issue of what God intended the relationship between Adam and Eve to be. "Helping" can be done by someone who has greater authority, someone who has equal authority, or someone who has lesser authority than the person being helped. For example, I can help my son do his homework.[19] Or I can help my neighbor move his sofa. Or my son can help me clean the garage. Yet the fact remains that the person doing the helping puts himself in a subordinate role to the person who has primary responsibility for carrying out the activity. Thus, even if I help my son with his homework, the primary responsibility for the homework remains his and not mine. I am the helper. And even when God helps us, with respect to the specific task at hand, He still holds us primarily responsible for the activity and accountable for what we do.

But Genesis 2 does not merely say that Eve functions as Adam's "helper" in one or two specific events. Rather, it says that God made Eve for the purpose of providing Adam with a helper, one who by virtue of creation would function as Adam's helper. "Then the Lord God said, 'It is not good that the man should be alone; I will make him a helper fit for him'" (Gen. 2:18). The Hebrew text can be translated quite literally as, "I will make *for him* (Hebrew *lô*) a helper fit for him." The apostle Paul understands this accurately, because in 1 Corinthians

11:9 (NASB) he writes, "for indeed man was not created for the woman's sake, but woman for the man's sake." Eve's role, and the purpose that God had in mind when He created her, was that she would be "for him . . . a helper."

Yet in the same text God emphasizes that she does not help Adam as one who is inferior to him. Rather, she is to be a helper "fit for him" and here the Hebrew word *kenegdô* means a helper "corresponding to" him, one that is "equal and adequate to himself ."[20] So Eve was created as a helper, but as a helper who was Adam's equal. She was created as one who differed from him, but who differed from him in ways that would exactly complement who Adam was.

7. *The conflict.* The curse brought a distortion of previous roles, not the introduction of new roles. After Adam and Eve sinned, God spoke the following words of judgment to Eve: "I will greatly increase your pains in childbearing; with pain you will give birth to children. Your *desire* will be for your husband, and he will *rule* over you" (Gen. 3:16, NIV, emphasis added).

The word translated "desire" is an unusual Hebrew word, *teshûqāh*. In this context and construction, it probably implies an aggressive desire, perhaps a desire to conquer or rule over, or else an urge or impulse for Eve to oppose her husband, an impulse to act "against" him. This sense is seen in the only other occurrence of *teshûqāh* in all the books of Moses, and in the only other occurrence of *teshûqāh* plus the preposition *'el* in the whole Bible. That occurrence of the word is in the very next chapter of Genesis, in 4:7. God says to Cain, "Sin is crouching at the door; and its *desire* is for you, but you must master it" (NASB). Here the sense is very clear. God pictures sin as a wild animal waiting outside Cain's door, waiting to attack him, even to pounce on him and overpower him. In that sense, sin's "desire," or "instinctive urge," is "against" him.[21]

The striking thing about that sentence is its remarkable parallel with Genesis 3:16. In the Hebrew text, six words are the same and in the same order in both verses. It is almost as if this other usage is put here by the author so that we would know how to understand the meaning of the term in Genesis 3:16. The expression in 4:7 has the sense of "desire, urge, impulse against" (or perhaps "desire to conquer, desire to rule over"), and that sense well fits Genesis 3:16.[22]

Some have assumed that the "desire" in Genesis 3:16 refers to sexual desire. But that is highly unlikely because (1) the entire Bible views sexual desire within marriage as something positive, not as something evil or something that God imposed as a judgment; and (2) surely Adam and Eve had sexual desire for one another prior to their sin, for God had told them to "be fruitful and multiply" (Gen. 1:28), and certainly in an unfallen world, along with the command, God would have given the desire that corresponded to it. So "your desire shall be for your husband" cannot refer to sexual desire. It is much more appropriate (to the context of a curse) to understand this as an aggressive desire against her husband, one that would bring her into conflict with him.

Then God says with regard to Adam, "and he shall rule over you" (Gen. 3:16). The word here translated "rule" is the Hebrew *māshal*. This term is common in the Old Testament and it regularly, if not always, refers to ruling by greater power or force or strength. It is used of human military or political rulers, such as Joseph ruling over the land of Egypt (Gen. 45:26), or the Philistines ruling over Israel (Judg. 14:4; 15:11), or Solomon ruling over all the kingdoms that he had conquered (1 Kings 4:21). It is also used to speak of God ruling over the sea (Ps. 89:9) or over the earth generally (Ps. 66:7). Sometimes it refers to oppressive rulers who cause the people under them to suffer (Neh. 9:37; Isa. 19:4). In any case, the word does not signify one who leads among equals but rather one who rules by virtue of power and strength, and sometimes even rules harshly and selfishly.

Once we understand these two terms, we can see much more clearly what was involved in the curse that God brought to Adam and Eve as punishment for their sins. One aspect of the curse was imposing pain on Adam's particular area of responsibility, raising food from the ground: "cursed is the ground because of you; in toil you shall eat of it all the days of your life; thorns and thistles it shall bring forth to you. . . . In the sweat of your face you shall eat bread till you return to the ground (Gen. 3:17-19). Another aspect was to impose pain on

Eve's particular area of responsibility, the bearing of children: "I will greatly multiply your pain in childbearing; in pain you shall bring forth children" (Gen. 3:16).

A third aspect of the curse was to introduce pain and conflict into the relationship between Adam and Eve. Prior to their sin, they had lived in perfect harmony, yet with a leadership role belonging to Adam as the head of his family. But after the Fall, God introduced conflict in that Eve would have an inward urging and impulsion to oppose Adam, to resist Adam's leadership (the verb *teshûqāh*), and Adam would respond with a rule over Eve that came from his greater strength and aggressiveness, a rule that was forceful and at times harsh (the verb *māshal*). There would be pain in tilling the ground, pain in bearing children, and pain and conflict in their relationship.

It is crucial at this point for us to realize that *we ourselves are never to try to increase or perpetuate the results of the curse.* We should never try to promote or advocate Genesis 3:16 as something good! In fact, the entire Bible following Genesis 3 is the story of God's working to overcome the effects of the curse that He in His justice imposed. Eventually God will bring in a new heaven and a new earth in which crops come forth abundantly from the ground (Isa. 35:1-2; Amos 9:13; Rom. 8:20-21) and in which there is no more pain or suffering (Rev. 21:4).

So we ourselves should never try to perpetuate the elements of the curse! We should not plant thorns and weeds in our gardens, but rather overcome them. We should do everything we can to alleviate the pain of childbirth for women. And we should do everything we can to undo conflict between men and women. Therefore Genesis 3:16 should never be used as a direct argument for male headship in marriage. But it does show us that the Fall brought about a distortion of previous roles, not the introduction of new roles. The distortion was that Eve would now rebel against her husband's authority and that Adam would misuse that authority to rule forcefully and even harshly over Eve.[23]

8. *The restoration.* When we come to the New Testament, salvation in Christ reaffirms the creation order. If the foregoing understanding

of Genesis 3:16 is correct, then we would expect to find in the New Testament a reversal of this curse, an undoing of the wife's hostile or aggressive impulses against her husband and the husband's response of harsh rule over his wife. In fact, that is exactly what we find. Colossians 3:18-19 states, "Wives, *be subject to your husbands,* as is fitting in the Lord. Husbands, *love your wives,* and do not be harsh with them."

This command is an undoing of the impulse to oppose (Hebrew *teshûqāh*) and the harsh rule (Hebrew *māshal*) that God imposed at the curse.

In the New Testament God reestablished the beauty of the relationship between Adam and Eve that existed from the moment they were created. Eve was subject to Adam as the head of the family. Adam loved his wife and was not harsh with her in his leadership. That is the pattern that Paul commands husbands and wives to follow.[24]

9. *The mystery.* Marriage from the beginning of creation was a picture of the relationship between Christ and the church. When the apostle Paul wishes to speak of the relationship between husband and wife, he does not look back to any sections of the Old Testament telling about the situation after sin came into the world. Rather, he looks all the way back to Genesis 2, prior to the Fall, and uses that creation order to speak of marriage: "'For this reason a man shall leave his father and mother and be joined to his wife, and the two shall become one flesh' [quoted from Gen. 2:24]. This mystery is a profound one, and I am saying that *it refers to Christ and the church*" (Eph. 5:31-32).

A "mystery" in Paul's writing is something that was understood only very faintly if at all in the Old Testament but is now made clearer in the New Testament. Here Paul makes clear the meaning of the "mystery" of marriage as God created it in the Garden of Eden. Paul is saying that the "mystery" of Adam and Eve, the meaning that was not previously understood, was that marriage "refers to Christ and the church." In other words, although Adam and Eve did not know it, their relationship represented the relationship between Christ and the church. They were created to represent that relationship, and that is what all marriages are supposed to do. In that relationship, Adam represents Christ and Eve represents the church, because "the husband is the head of the wife as Christ is the head of the church" (Eph. 5:23).

The relationship between Christ and the church is not culturally variable. It is the same for all generations. And it is not reversible. There is a leadership or headship role that belongs to Christ, a role that the church does not have. Similarly, in marriage as God created it to be, there is a leadership role for the husband that the wife does not have. And for our purposes it is important to notice that this relationship was there from the beginning of creation, in the beautiful marriage between Adam and Eve in the garden.

10. *The parallel with the Trinity.* The equality, differences, and unity between men and women reflect the equality, differences, and unity in the Trinity. Though I list this here as the tenth indication that there were differences in roles between men and women from creation, I will not explain it at this point but in "Key Issue 3" below.

Conclusion. Here then are at least ten indications of differences in the roles of men and women before the Fall. Some of these indications are not as forceful as others, though all have some weight. Some "whisper" male headship, others shout it clearly. But they form a cumulative case showing that Adam and Eve had distinct roles before the Fall, and that this was God's purpose in creating them.

How Do Equality and Headship Work in Practice?

I would like to say something about how male-female equality combined with male headship works out in practice. The situation I know best is my own marriage, so I will speak about that briefly.

Margaret and I talk frequently and at length about many decisions, whether large ones (such as buying a house or a car) or small ones (such as where we should go for a walk together). I often defer to her wishes, and she often defers to mine. In almost every case, each of us has some wisdom and insight that the other does not have, and we have learned to listen to each other and to place much trust in each other's judgment. Usually we reach agreement on the decision. Very seldom will I do something that she does not think to be wise. She prays, she loves God, she is sensitive to the Lord's leading and direction, and I greatly respect her and the wisdom God gives her.

But in every decision, whether large or small, and whether we have reached agreement or not, the responsibility to make the decision still rests with me. I do not agree with those who say that male headship only makes a difference once in ten years or so when a husband and wife can't reach agreement. I think that male headship makes a difference in every decision that the couple makes every day of their married life. If there is genuine male headship, there is a quiet, subtle acknowledgment that the focus of the decision-making process is the husband, not the wife. And even though there will often be much discussion, and there should be much mutual respect and consideration of each other, yet ultimately the responsibility to make the decision rests with the husband. And so in our marriage, the responsibility to make the decision rests with me.[25]

This is not because I am wiser or a more gifted leader. It is because I am the husband, and God has given me that responsibility. In the face of cultural pressures to the contrary, I will not forsake this male headship, I will not deny it, I will not be embarrassed by it.

It is God-given. It is very good. It brings peace and joy to our marriage, and both Margaret and I are thankful for it.

Yet there are dangers of distortion in one direction or another. Putting this biblical pattern into practice in our daily lives is a challenge, because we can err in one direction or the other. There are errors of passivity and errors of aggressiveness. This can be seen in the following chart:

	Errors of passivity	Biblical ideal	Errors of aggressiveness
Husband	Wimp	Loving, humble headship	Tyrant
Wife	Doormat	Joyful, intelligent submission	Usurper

The biblical ideal, in the center column, is loving, humble headship on the part of the husband, following Ephesians 5:23-33. The biblical ideal on the part of the wife is joyful, intelligent submission to and support of her husband's leadership, in accordance with Ephesians 5:22-24 and 31-33.

On the right side of the chart are the errors of aggressiveness, which had their beginning in Genesis 3:16. The husband can become selfish, harsh, and domineering, and can act like a tyrant. This is not biblical headship but a tragic distortion of it. A wife can also demonstrate errors of aggressiveness when she resists and continually struggles against her husband's leadership, not supporting it but fighting against it and creating conflict every step of the way. She can become a usurper, which is a tragic distortion of the biblical pattern of equality in the image of God.

On the left side of the chart are the opposite errors, the errors of passivity. A husband can abdicate leadership and neglect his responsibilities. The children are not disciplined, and he sits and watches television and does nothing. The family is not going to church regularly and he does nothing. The family keeps going further into debt and he closes his eyes to it. Some relative or friend is verbally harassing his wife and he is silent. This also is a tragic distortion of the biblical pattern. He has become a "wimp."

A wife can also commit errors of passivity. Rather than participating actively in family decisions, rather than contributing her much needed wisdom and insight, her only response to every situation is, "Yes, dear, whatever you say." She knows her husband and her children are doing wrong and she says nothing. Or her husband becomes verbally or physically abusive, and she never objects to him, never seeks church discipline or civil governmental intervention to bring an end to the abuse. Or she never really expresses her own preferences with regard to friendships or family vacations, or her own opinions regarding people or events. She thinks that this is what is required in order to be "submissive" to her husband. But this also is a tragic distortion of biblical patterns. She has become a "doormat."

Now we all have different backgrounds, personalities, and temperaments. We also have different areas of life in which sanctification is less complete. Therefore some of us tend to be more prone toward errors of aggressiveness while others tend to be more prone toward errors of passivity. We can even fall into errors of aggressiveness in our own homes and into errors of passivity when we visit our in-laws! Or it can be just the other way around. In order to maintain a healthy biblical balance, we need to keep reading God's Word each day, continue to pray for God's help each day, and continue to follow in obedience to God's Word as best we can.

The Man's Responsibility to Provide for and to Protect, and the Woman's Responsibility to Care for the Home and to Nurture Children

There are other differences in roles in addition to headship and submission. Two other aspects of a man's headship in marriage are his responsibilities to *provide for* his wife and family and to *protect* them. A corresponding responsibility on the part of the wife is to have primary responsibility to care for home and children. Each can help the other, but each have their primary responsibilities, which are not shared equally. These responsibilities are mentioned in both the Danvers Statement and the Southern Baptist Convention/Campus Crusade for Christ statement. I will not discuss these in detail, but simply note that these additional aspects of the differing roles are established in Scripture.

Biblical support for the husband having the primary responsibility to provide for his family and for the wife having primary responsibility to care for the household and children is found in Genesis 2:15 with 2:18-23; 3:16-17 (Eve is assumed to have the primary responsibility for childbearing, but Adam for tilling the ground to raise food; and pain is introduced into both of their areas of responsibility); Proverbs 31:10-31, especially vv. 13, 15, 21, 27; Isaiah 4:1 (shame at the tragic undoing of the normal order); 1 Timothy 5:8 (the Greek text does not specify any "man," but in the historical context that would have been the assumed referent except for unusual situations such as a household with no father); 1 Timothy 5:10; 1 Timothy 5:3-16 (widows, not widowers, are to be supported by the church); Titus 2:5. I believe that a wife's created role as a "helper fit for him" (Gen. 2:18) also supports this distinction of roles. I do not think a wife would be fulfilling her role as "helper" if she became the permanent primary breadwinner, for then the husband would be the primary "helper."

Biblical support for the idea that the man has the primary responsibility to protect his family is found in Deuteronomy 20:7-8 (men, not women, go forth to war—here and in many Old Testament passages); Deuteronomy 24:5; Joshua 1:14; Judges 4:8-10 (Barak does not get the glory, because he insisted that a woman accompany him into battle); Nehemiah 4:13-14 (the people are to fight for their brothers, homes, wives, and children, but it does not say they are to fight for their husbands!); Jeremiah 50:37 (it is the disgrace of a nation when its warriors become women); Nahum 3:13 ("Behold, your troops are women in your midst" is a taunt of derision); Matthew 2:13-14 (Joseph is told to protect Mary and the infant Jesus by taking them to Egypt); Ephesians 5:25 (a husband's love should extend even to a willingness to lay down his life for his wife, something many soldiers in battle have done throughout history to protect their families and homelands); 1 Peter 3:7 (a wife is a "weaker vessel," and therefore the husband, as generally stronger, has a greater responsibility to use his strength to protect his wife).

In addition, there is the complete absence of evidence from the other side. Nowhere can we find Scripture encouraging women to be the primary means of support while their husbands care for the house and children. Nowhere can we find Scripture encouraging women to be the primary protectors of their husbands. Certainly women can help in these roles as time and circumstances allow (Gen. 2:18-23), but they are not the ones primarily responsible for them.

Finally, there is the evidence of the internal testimony from both men's and women's hearts. There is something in a man that says, "I don't want to be dependent on a woman to provide for me in the long term. I want to be the one responsible to provide for the family, the one my wife looks to and depends on for support." Personally, I have never met a man who does not feel some measure of shame at the idea of being supported by his wife in the long term. (I recognize that in many families there is a temporary reversal of roles due to involuntary unemployment or while the husband is getting further education for his career, and in those circumstances these are entirely appropriate arrangements; yet the longer they go on, the more strain they put on a marriage. I also recognize that permanent disability on the part of the husband, or the absence of a husband in the home, can create a necessity for the wife to be the primary provider, but every family in which that happens will testify to the unusual stress it brings and the fact that they wish it did not have to be so.) On the other hand, there is something in a woman that says, "I want my husband to provide for me, to give me the security of knowing that we will have enough to buy groceries and pay the bills. It feels right to me to look to him and depend on him for that responsibility." Personally, I have never met a woman who did not want her husband to provide that sense of security for her.[26]

Some Egalitarian Objections to Male Headship in Marriage

Egalitarians raise a number of objections to the idea that men and women have different roles in marriage as part of the created order, different roles that should find expression in marriages today as well. Here are three of the most common objections:

1. Galatians 3:28 abolishes role distinctions in marriage.

2. "Mutual submission" in Ephesians 5:21 nullifies male authority in marriage.

3. "The husband is the head of the wife" (Eph. 5:23) does not indicate authority for the husband because "head" means "source" or something else, but not "person in authority."

I will consider these three objections briefly at this point, since they are treated more extensively elsewhere.[27]

Objection 1: Galatians 3:28 abolishes role distinctions in marriage.

In this verse, Paul says, "There is neither Jew nor Greek, there is neither slave nor free, there is neither male nor female; for you are all one in Christ Jesus." Egalitarians frequently claim that if there is "neither male nor female" then distinctions in role based on our gender are abolished because we are now all "one in Christ Jesus."

But this is not what the verse says. To say that we are "one" means that we are *united,* that there should be no factions or divisions among us, and, that there should be no sense of pride and superiority or jealousy and inferiority between these groups (who viewed themselves as so distinct in the ancient world). Jews should no longer think themselves superior to Greeks, freed men should no longer think themselves superior to slaves, and men should no longer think themselves superior to women. They are all parts of one body in Christ, and all share in equal value and dignity as members of one body in Christ.

As Richard Hove has demonstrated in detail,[28] when the Bible says that several things are "one," it never joins things that are exactly the same. Rather, it says that things that are different, things that are diverse, share some kind of unity. So, in Romans 12:4-5, we read, "For as in one body we have many members, and all the members do not have the same function, so we, though many, *are one body* in Christ, and individually members one of another." Paul does not mean to say that all the members of the body are the same, for, as anyone can see, a body has hands and feet and eyes and ears, and the different "members" have different functions, though they are one body.

Similarly, using the same construction,[29] Paul can say, "Now he who plants and he who waters *are one;* but each will receive his own reward according to his own labor" (1 Cor. 3:8, NASB). Planting and watering are two different activities done by different persons in Paul's example. They are not reduced to "sameness," nor are they required to act in exactly the same way, but they are still "one" because they have a kind of unity of purpose and goal. And so Galatians 3:28 simply says that we have a special kind of unity in the body of Christ. Our differences as male and female are not obliterated by this unity, but the unity is beautiful in God's sight particularly because it is a unity that comes about from different kinds of people.

Surely this verse cannot abolish all differences between men and women. Paul himself elsewhere commands husbands and wives to act differently according to their different roles, and marriage in Scripture from beginning to end is intended by God to be only between one man and one woman, not between one man and another man or one woman and another woman. If Galatians 3:28 truly abolished all differences between men and women, then how could anyone say that homosexual marriage was wrong? But homosexual conduct is surely forbidden by Scripture (Rom. 1:26-27; 1 Cor. 6:9; 1 Tim. 1:10). (Egalitarians within the evangelical world agree that homosexual conduct is prohibited by Scripture.) Clearly, Galatians 3:28 does not abolish differences in roles between men and women.

> *Objection 2: "Mutual submission" in Ephesians 5:21 nullifies male authority in marriage.*

Ephesians 5:21 says, "Be subject to one another out of reverence for Christ." Egalitarians say that this teaches "mutual submission," which means that just as wives have to submit to their husbands, *so husbands have to submit to their wives.* Doesn't the text say that we have to submit "to one another," they ask? And doesn't this means that there is no unique kind of submission that a wife owes to her husband, and no unique kind of authority that a husband has over his wife? Sometimes egalitarians will say something like this: "Of course I believe that a wife should be subject to her husband. And a husband should also be subject to his wife." Or, "I will be subject to my husband as soon as he is subject to me." And so, as egalitarians understand Ephesians 5:21, there is no difference in roles between men and women. There is no unique leadership role, no unique authority, for the husband. There is simply "mutual submission."[30]

I want to affirm, of course, that people can mean different things by "mutual submission." There is a sense of the phrase "mutual submission" that is different from an egalitarian view and that does not nullify the husband's authority within marriage. For instance, if "mutual submission" means being considerate of one another, and caring for one another's needs, and being thoughtful of one another, then of course I would agree that "mutual submission" is a good thing.

However, egalitarians mean something so different by this phrase, and they have used this phrase so often to nullify male authority within marriage, that I think the expression "mutual submission" only leads to confusion.[31]

In previous generations some people did speak about "mutual submission," but never in the sense in which egalitarians today understand it. In his study of the history of the interpretation of Ephesians 5:21, Daniel Doriani has demonstrated that a number of earlier writers thought that there was a kind of "mutual submission" taught in the verse, but that such "submission" took very different forms for those *in authority* and for those *under authority.* They took it to mean that those in authority should govern wisely and with sacrificial concern for those under their authority. But Doriani found no author in the history of the church prior to the advent of feminism in the last half of the twentieth century who thought that "be subject to one another" in Ephesians 5:21 nullified the authority of the husband within marriage.[32]

What is wrong with understanding Ephesians 5:21 to teach "mutual submission"? There are at least four reasons why I think this understanding is incorrect.

(1) The context of this verse specifies the kind of submission Paul has in mind. Paul explains that wives are to be subject to their husbands (Eph. 5:22-23), children are to be subject to their parents (Eph. 6:1-3), and slaves (or bondservants) are to be subject to their masters (Eph. 6:5-8). These relationships are never reversed. He does not tell husbands to be subject to wives, or parents to be subject to their children (thus nullifying all parental authority!), or masters to be subject to their servants. In fact, Paul does not tell husbands and wives generally to be subject to each other, nor does he tell wives to be subject to other people's husbands! He says, "Wives, be subject to *your own* husbands, as to the Lord" (Eph. 5:22, NASB).[33]

(2) The meaning of "be subject to" (*hypotassō*). When we look at the word that Paul used when he said, "Be subject to one another" (Eph. 5:21), we find that this word (Greek *hypotassō*) in the New

Testament is always used of submission to an authority. Here are some examples:

• Jesus was subject ("obedient") to the authority of his parents (Luke 2:51).

• Demons were "subject to" the disciples (Luke 10:17; it is clear that the meaning "be considerate of, be thoughtful toward" cannot fit here, for the demons were certainly not considerate of or thoughtful toward the disciples!).

• Citizens are to be "subject to" the governing authorities (Rom. 13:1, 5; see also Titus 3:1; 1 Pet. 2:13).

• The universe is "in subjection" to Christ (1 Cor. 15:27; see also Eph. 1:22).

• Angels and other spiritual beings are "subject to" Christ (1 Pet. 3:22).

• Christ is "subjected to" God the Father (1 Cor. 15:28).

• Church members are to be "subject to" the elders in the church (1 Pet. 5:5[34]).

. • Wives are told to be "subject to" their husbands (Eph. 5:22, 24; Col. 3:18; Titus 2:5, 1 Pet. 3:5).

• The church is "subject to" Christ (Eph. 5:24).

• Servants are to be "subject to" their masters (Titus 2:9; 1 Pet. 2:18).

• Christians are to be "subject to" God (Heb. 12:9; James 4:7).

This list should demonstrate clearly that to "be subject to" someone, in the sense that is signified by the word *hypotassō,* always means to be subject to the authority of that other person. In all of these examples, there is no exception. The subjection is one-directional and the person who is under authority is subject to the person who has authority over him or her. The relationships indicated by the word *hypotassō* simply do not envision relationships where the authority is mutual, or where it is reciprocal, or where it is reversed. It is only one-directional.

(3) The lack of evidence for the egalitarian meaning. In all of this controversy over roles for men and women, no one has yet produced any examples in ancient Greek literature (either inside or outside the New Testament) where *hypotassō* is applied to a relationship between

persons where it does not carry the sense of being subject to an authority.

I have been asking a particular question in one form or another for fifteen years now (since I first asked it in the plenary sessions of the 1986 meetings of the Evangelical Theological Society in Atlanta, Georgia), and I have not received an answer yet. The question is addressed to egalitarians, and the question is this: "Why should we assign to *hypotassō* in the New Testament a meaning ('defer to' or 'be considerate of, be thoughtful of') that it is nowhere attested to have, and that no Greek lexicon has ever assigned to it, and that empties it of a meaning (one-directional submission to an authority) which it always has when speaking of relationships between persons?" The question remains unanswered.[35]

(4) The meaning of "one another" (in "be subject to one another"). The Greek term translated "one another" (*allēlous*) can have two different meanings. Sometimes in the New Testament it means something like "everyone to everyone," as in verses like John 13:34, "A new commandment I give to you, that you *love one another.*" Everyone would agree that this means that all Christians are to love all other Christians. It has the sense "everyone to everyone."

But at other times in the New Testament it means *"some* to others." For example, in Revelation 6:4, the rider on the red horse "was permitted to take peace from the earth so that men should *slay one another."* This does not mean that each person first got killed and then got back up and killed the one who had murdered him! It simply means that some killed others. Here the word *allēlous* does not mean "everyone to everyone" but "some to others." We see a similar example in Galatians 6:2, "Bear *one another's* burdens, and so fulfill the law of Christ." Here Paul does not mean that everybody should switch burdens with everybody else, but only that some who are more able should bear the burdens of others who are less able to bear their burdens. And in 1 Corinthians 11:33, Paul says, "When you come together to eat, *wait for one another."* This does not mean that those who come early should wait for those who are late and those who are late should wait for those who are there early! It only means that those who are early should wait for the others, who are late. Here again, *allēlous* means "some to others," or "some" are to wait for "others." The New Testament has many other examples of this (e.g., Luke 2:14; 21:1; 24:32).

Therefore, "be subject to one another" in Ephesians 5:21 can take the sense "some be subject to others" if the context fits or requires this meaning. And, as we have seen, the word translated "be subject to" (*hypotassō*) requires this sense, because it is never used to speak of a reciprocal relationship between persons but always signifies one-directional submission to an authority. Therefore we can paraphrase Ephesians 5:21 as, "Be subject to others in the church who are in positions of authority over you."[36]

No idea of "mutual submission" is taught in Ephesians 5:21. The idea itself is self-contradictory if *hypotassō* means here (as it does everywhere else) "be subject to an authority."

With respect to your own churches, if you want to add a statement on men and women in marriage to your governing document or publish it as a policy statement (as did the Southern Baptist Convention and Campus Crusade for Christ), and if in the process someone proposes to add the phrase "mutual submission" to the document, I urge you strongly not to agree to it. In the sense that egalitarians understand the phrase "mutual submission," the idea is found nowhere in Scripture, and it actually nullifies the teaching of significant passages of Scripture.

Yet, I must add one further word of caution. Some people who hold a fully complementarian view of marriage do use the phrase "mutual submission" and intend it in a way that does not nullify male leadership in marriage. I have found that some people who want to use this language may simply have genuine concerns that men do not act like "dictators" or "tyrants" in their marriages. If this is what they are seeking to guard against by the phrase "mutual submission," then I suggest trying this alternative wording, which is found in the Campus Crusade for Christ statement:

> In a marriage lived according to these truths, the love between husband and wife will show itself in listening to each other's view-

points, valuing each others' gifts, wisdom, and desires, honoring one another in public and in private, and always seeking to bring benefit, not harm, to one another.

Objection 3: "The husband is the head of the wife" does not indicate author-ity for the husband, because "head" means "source" or something else, but not "person in authority."

In 1 Corinthians 11:3, Paul says, "Now I want you to realize that the head [Greek *kephalē*] of every man is Christ, the head of a woman is her husband, and the head of Christ is God." And Ephesians 5:23 reads, "For the husband is the head of the wife as Christ is the head of the church, his body, and is himself its Savior." It is important to real-ize the decisive significance of these verses, and particularly of Ephesians 5:23, for the current controversy. If the word "head" means "person in authority over," then there is a unique authority that belongs to the husband in marriage and which parallels Christ's authority over the church. If so, then the egalitarians have lost the debate.[37]

So what have egalitarians done to give a different meaning to the statement, "The husband is the head of the wife as Christ is the head of the church"? The most common approach has been to say that the word translated "head" (Greek *kephalē*) does not mean "person in authority over" but has some other meaning, especially "source." Thus, the husband is the source of the wife (an allusion to the creation of Eve from Adam's side in Genesis 2), as Christ is the source of the church. The problem of this interpretation is that it does not fit the evidence.

In 1985, I looked up 2,336 examples of the word "head" (*kephalē*) in ancient Greek literature, using texts from Homer in the eighth cen-tury B.C. up to some church fathers in the fourth century A.D. I found that in those texts *kephalē* was applied to many people in authority (when it was used in a metaphorical sense to say that person A was the head of person or persons B), but it was never applied to a person without governing authority.[38] In these texts, I found examples such as the following:

- The king of Egypt is called "head" of the nation.
- The general of an army is called "head" of the army.

- The Roman emperor is called the "head" of the people.
- The god Zeus is called the "head" of all things.
- David as king of Israel is called the "head" of the people.
- The leaders of the tribes of Israel are called "heads" of the tribes.
- The husband is the "head" of the wife.
- Christ is the "head" of the church.
- God, the Father, is the "head" of Christ.

No one has yet produced one text in ancient Greek literature (from the eighth century B.C. to the fourth century A.D.) where a person is called the *kephalē* ("head") of another person or group and that person is not the one in authority over that other person or group. Now sixteen years after the publication of my 1985 study, the alleged meaning "source without authority" has still not been supported with any citation of any text in ancient Greek literature. More than fifty examples of *kephalē* meaning "ruler, authority over" have been found, but no examples of the meaning "source without authority."

The question is, why should we give *kephalē* in the New Testament a sense which, when applied to persons, no Greek lexicon has ever given to it? The egalitarian interpretation of this word is also a novel one in the history of the church. So far as I know, no one in the history of the church before the 1970s ever claimed that *kephalē* in Ephesians 5:23 meant "source" in a way that denied leadership or authority to the husband.[39] More recently, we have a letter from a scholar who by virtue of position and reputation may rightly be called the greatest Greek lexicographer alive in the world today, P. G. W. Glare of Oxford. Glare is the editor of the *Liddell-Scott Greek-English Lexicon: Supplement* (Oxford: Clarendon Press, 1996).

In a personal letter, which he has allowed me to quote, Glare says:

Dear Professor Grudem,
    · Thank you for sending me the copy of your article on κεφαλή. The entry under this word in LSJ is not very satisfactory. Perhaps I could draw your attention to a section of *Lexicographica Graeca* by Dr John Chadwick (OUP 1996), though he does not deal in detail with the Septuagint and NT material. I was unable to revise the longer articles in LSJ when I was preparing the latest *Supplement*,

since I did not have the financial resources to carry out a full-scale revision.

I have no time at the moment to discuss all your examples individually and in any case I am in broad agreement with your conclusions. I might just make one or two generalizations. κεφαλή is the word normally used to translate the Hebrew ראש and this *does seem frequently to denote leader or chief* without much reference to its original anatomical sense, and *here it seems perverse to deny authority. The supposed sense 'source' of course does not exist* and it was at least unwise of Liddell and Scott to mention the word. At the most they should have said 'applied to the source of a river in respect of its position in its (the river's) course'.

By NT times the Septuagint had been well established and one would only expect that a usage found frequently in it would come easily to such a writer as St. Paul. Where I would agree with Cervin is that in many of the examples, and I think all the Plutarch ones, we are dealing with similes or comparisons and the word itself is used in a literal sense. Here we are faced with the inadequacies of LSJ. If they had clearly distinguished between, for example, 'the head as the seat of the intellect and emotions (and therefore the director of the body's actions)' and 'the head as the extremity of the human or animal body' and so on, these figurative examples would naturally be attached to the end of the section they belong to and the author's intention would be clear. I hasten to add that in most cases the sense of the head as being the controlling agent is the one required and that *the idea of preeminence seems to me to be quite unsuitable,* and that there are still cases where κεφαλή can be understood, as in the Septuagint, in its transferred sense of head or leader.

Once again, thank you for sending me the article. I shall file it in the hope that one day we will be able to embark on a more thorough revision of the lexicon.

Yours sincerely,

Peter Glare[40]

So this egalitarian objection also fails to be convincing, and we are right to conclude that the Bible gives husbands the responsibility of a unique leadership role, a unique authority, in the marriage.

KEY ISSUE 3: THE EQUALITY AND DIFFERENCES BETWEEN
MEN AND WOMEN REFLECT THE EQUALITY AND
DIFFERENCES IN THE TRINITY

This point is at the heart of the controversy, and it shows why much more is at stake than the meaning of one or two words or verses in the Bible. Much more is at stake even than how we live in our marriages. Here we are talking about the nature of God Himself.

In 1 Corinthians 11:3 Paul writes, "But I want you to understand that the head of every man is Christ, the head of a woman is her husband, and the head of Christ is God." In this verse, the word "head" refers to one who is in a position of authority over the other, as this Greek word (*kephalē*) uniformly does whenever it is used in ancient literature to say that one person is "head of" another person or group.[41] So Paul is here referring to a relationship of authority between God the Father and God the Son, and he is making a parallel between that relationship in the Trinity and the relationship between the husband and wife in marriage. This is an important parallel because it shows that there can be equality and differences between persons at the same time. We can illustrate that in the following diagram, where the arrows indicate authority over the person to whom the arrow points:

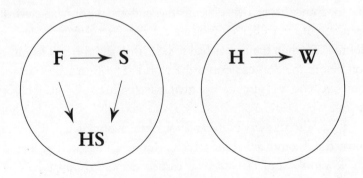

The Father and Son are equal in diety and in value, just as husband and wife are equal in personhood and in value. Yet the Father has authority over the Son, as the husband has authority over the wife.

Just as the Father and Son are equal in deity and equal in all their attributes, but different in role, the husband and wife are equal in personhood and value but different in the roles that God has given them. Just as God the Son is eternally subject to the authority of God the Father, so God has planned that wives would be subject to the authority of their husbands.

Scripture frequently speaks of the Father-Son relationship within the Trinity, a relationship in which the Father "gave" His only Son (John 3:16) and "sent" the Son into the world (John 3:17, 34; 4:34; 8:42; Gal. 4:4; and so on), a relationship in which the Father "predestined" us to be conformed to the image of His Son (Rom. 8:29; compare 1 Pet. 1:2) and "chose us" in the Son "before the foundation of the world" (Eph. 1:4). The Son is obedient to the commands of the Father (John 12:49) and says that He comes to do "the will of him who sent me" (John 4:34; 6:38). These relationships are never reversed. Never does Scripture say that the Son sends the Father, or that the Holy Spirit sends the Father or the Son, or that the Father obeys the commands of the Son or the Holy Spirit. Never does Scripture say that the Son predestined us to be conformed to the image of the Father. The role of planning, directing, sending, and commanding the Son belongs to the Father only.

These relationships are eternal, for the Father predestined us in the Son "before the foundation of the world" (Eph. 1:4), requiring that the Father has eternally been Father and that the Son has eternally been Son. If the Father's love is seen in that He "gave his only Son" (John 3:16), then the Father had to be Father and the Son had to be Son before the Son came into the world. The Father did not give someone who was just another divine person in the Trinity. He gave the one who was His only Son, one who eternally had been His Son.

It was also this way in the creation of the world, where the Father initiated and commanded and created "through" the Son. The Son was the powerful Word of God who carried out the commands of the Father, for "all things were made through him" (John 1:3). The Son is the one "through whom" God created the world (Heb. 1:2). All things were created by the Father working through the Son, for "there is one God, the Father, *from* whom are all things . . . and one Lord, Jesus Christ, *through* whom are all things" (1 Cor. 8:6). Nowhere does Scripture reverse this and say that the Son created "through" the Father.

The Son sits at the Father's right hand (Rom. 8:34; Heb. 1:3, 13; 1 Pet. 3:22); the Father does not sit at the Son's right hand. And for all eternity, the Son will be subject to the Father, for after the last enemy, death, is destroyed, "the Son himself will also be subjected to him who put all things under him, that God may be everything to every one" (1 Cor. 15:28).

We see from these passages, then, that the *idea of headship and submission within a personal relationship* did not begin with the Council on Biblical Manhood and Womanhood in 1987. Nor did it begin with some writings of the apostle Paul in the first century. Nor did it begin with a few patriarchal men in a patriarchal society in the Old Testament. Nor did it begin with Adam and Eve's fall into sin in Genesis 3. In fact, the idea of headship and submission did not even begin with the creation of Adam and Eve. It existed *before creation,* in the relationship between the Father and Son in the Trinity. The Father has eternally had a leadership role, an authority to initiate and direct, that the Son does not have. Similarly, the Holy Spirit is subject to both the Father and Son and plays yet a different role in creation and in the work of salvation.

When did the idea of headship and submission begin, then? *The idea of headship and submission never began!* It has *always existed* in the eternal nature of God Himself. And in this most basic of all authority relationships, authority is not based on gifts or ability (for the Father, Son, and Holy Spirit are equal in attributes and perfections); it is just there. Authority belongs to the Father, not because He is wiser or because He is a more skillful leader, but just because He is the Father. Authority and submission between the Father and the Son, and between both Father and Son and the Holy Spirit, is the fundamental difference in the persons of the Trinity. They don't differ in any attributes, but in how They relate to each other. And that relationship is one of leadership and authority on the one hand and voluntary, willing, joyful submission to that authority on the other hand. We can learn from this that submission to a rightful authority is a noble virtue. It is a privilege. It is something good and desirable. It is the virtue that has been demonstrated by the eternal Son of God *forever*. It is His glory, the glory of the Son as He relates to His Father.

In modern society, we tend to think that if you are a person who has authority over another, that's a good thing, but if you are the one who has to submit to an authority, that's a bad thing. But that is the world's viewpoint, and it is not true. Submission to a rightful authority is a good and noble and wonderful thing, because it reflects the interpersonal relationships within God Himself. We can say, then, that a relationship of authority and submission between equals, with mutual giving of honor, is the most fundamental and most glorious interpersonal relationship in the universe. Such a relationship allows there to be interpersonal differences without "better" or "worse," without "more important" and "less important."

When we begin to dislike *the very idea of authority and submission*— not distortions and abuses, but the very idea—we are tampering with something very deep. We are beginning to dislike God Himself. This truth about the Trinity creates a problem for egalitarians within the church. They try to force people to choose between equality and authority. They say, if you have male headship, then you can't be equal. Or if you are equal, then you can't have male headship. And our response is that you can have both: Just look at the Trinity. Within the being of God, you have both equality and authority.

In reply to this, egalitarians should have said, "Okay, we agree on this much. In God you can have equality and differences at the same time." In fact, some egalitarians have said this.[42] But some prominent egalitarians have taken a different direction, one that is very troubling. Both Gilbert Bilezikian and Stanley Grenz have now written that they think there is "mutual submission" within the Trinity. They say that the Father also submits to the Son.[43] This is their affirmation, though no passage of Scripture affirms such a relationship and though this has never been the orthodox teaching of the Christian church throughout 2,000 years. But so deep is their commitment to an egalitarian view of men and women within marriage that they will modify the doctrine of the Trinity, and remake the Trinity in the image of egalitarian marriage, if it seems necessary in order to maintain their position.

KEY ISSUE 4: THE EQUALITY AND DIFFERENCES BETWEEN MEN AND WOMEN ARE VERY GOOD

In today's culture we might be embarrassed to talk about God-given differences between men and women. We don't want to be attacked or laughed at. Perhaps we fear that someone will take offense. (However, there is more acknowledgment of male/female differences in the general culture today than there was a few years ago. A number of secular books, such as John Gray's *Men Are from Mars, Women Are from Venus,* have once again made it acceptable to talk about at least some differences between men and women, though the idea of a husband's authority and the wife's submission within marriage still seems to be taboo in the general culture.)[44] Nevertheless, the way God created us as men and women, equal in His image and different in roles, was "very good." This fundamental statement of our excellence is found in Genesis 1:31: "And God saw everything that he had made, and behold, *it was very good.*" And if it is "very good," then we can make some other observations about the created order.

This created order is fair. Egalitarians argue that it is "not fair" for men to have a leadership role in the family simply because they are men. But if this difference is based on God's assignment of roles from the beginning, then it is fair. Does the Son say to the Father, "It's not fair for You to be in charge simply because You are the Father"? Does the Son say to the Father, "You've been in charge for fifteen billion years, and now it's My turn for the next fifteen billion"? Absolutely not! Rather, He fulfilled the Psalm that said, "I desire to do your will, O my God; your law is within my heart" (Ps. 40:8, ESV; compare Heb. 10:7). And of His relationship with the Father, He said, "I always do what is pleasing to him" (John 8:29), and, "I have come down from heaven, not to do my own will, but the will of him who sent me" (John 6:38). The order of relationships within the Trinity is fair. And the order of relationships established by God for marriage is fair.

This created order is also best for us. It is best because it comes from an all-wise Creator. This created order truly honors men and women. It does not lead to abuse; it guards against it, because both men and women are equal in value before God. It does not suppress women's gifts and wisdom and insight; it encourages them.

This created order is also a mystery. I have been married to one very wonderful woman for thirty-two years, but I don't completely understand her. Just when I think I understand her, she surprises me again. Marriage is a challenge! And it's also very fun. But in our relationships with each other as men and women there will always be elements of surprise, always elements of mystery, always aspects of difference that we will not fully understand but simply enjoy.

This created order is beautiful. God took delight in it and thought it was "very good." When it is functioning in the way that God intended, we will enjoy this relationship and delight in it, because there is a God-like quality about it. And in fact, though some elements of society have been pushing in the opposite direction for several decades, there is much evidence from "natural law"—from our observation of the world and our inner sense of right and wrong—that men and women have a sense that different roles within marriage are right. This is what we meant when we said in the Danvers Statement, "Distinctions in masculine and feminine roles are ordained by God and should find an echo in every human heart" (Affirmation Two). God's created order for marriage is beautiful because it is God's way to bring amazing *unity* to people who are so *different,* as men and women are.

The beauty of God's created order for marriage also finds expression in our sexuality within marriage. "Therefore a man shall leave his father and his mother and hold fast to his wife, and they shall become one flesh" (Gen. 2:24, ESV). From the beginning, God designed our sexuality so that it reflects unity and differences and beauty all at the same time. As husband and wife, we are most attracted to the parts of each other that are the most different. Our deepest unity—physical and emotional and spiritual unity—comes at the point where we are most different. In our physical union as God intended it, there is no dehumanization of women and no emasculation of men, but there is equality and honor for both the husband and the wife. And there is our deepest human joy and our deepest expression of unity.

This means that sexuality within marriage is precious to God. It is designed by Him to show *equality* and *difference* and *unity* all at the same time. It is a great mystery how this can be so, and it is also a great blessing and joy. Moreover, God has ordained that from that sexual union comes the most amazing, the most astounding event—the creation of a new human being in the image of God.

Within this most intimate of human relationships, we show equality and difference and unity and much God-likeness all at once. Glory be to God!

Key Issue 5: This Is a Matter of Obedience to the Bible

Why did the Southern Baptist Convention in June 1998, for the first time since 1963, add to their statement of faith that men and women are equal in God's image but different in their roles in marriage?[45] Why, shortly after that, did more than a hundred Christian leaders sign a full-page ad in *USA Today* saying, "Southern Baptists . . . you are right! We stand with you!"[46] Why did Campus Crusade for Christ, after forty years of no change in their doctrinal policies, endorse a similar statement as the policy of their organization in 1999?[47] Clearly, many Christian leaders are beginning to say, "The egalitarian view just cannot be proven from Scripture."

Twenty-five years ago there were many questions of differences in interpretation, and both the egalitarian position and the complementarian position were found within evangelical groups. Over the last twenty-five years, we have seen extensive discussion and argument of both views, and we have seen hundreds of articles and books published. But it seems to me that people are beginning to look at the situation differently. The egalitarian viewpoint, which was novel within evangelicalism twenty-five years ago, has had great opportunity to defend itself. The arguments are all out on the table, and the detailed studies of words of the Bible, the technical questions of grammar, and the extensive studies of background literature and history have been carried out. There are dozens and dozens of egalitarian books denying differences in male and female roles within marriage, but they now seem to be repeating the same arguments over and over. The egalitarians have not had any new breakthroughs, any new discoveries that lend any substantial strength to their position.

It seems to me that many people in leadership are now deciding that the egalitarian view is simply not what the Bible teaches. And they are deciding that it will not be taught in their churches, so they add clauses to that effect to their statements of faith. Then the controversy is essentially over, for that group at least, for the next ten or twenty years.

James Dobson saw the wisdom of this. After Campus Crusade announced its policy in June 1999, Dobson's newsletter in September 1999, on the front page, said, "We applaud our friends at Campus Crusade for taking this courageous stance." He quoted the statement in full and then said, "It is our prayer that additional denominations and parachurch organizations will join with SBC in adopting this statement on marriage and the family. Now is the time for Christian people to identify themselves unreservedly with the truths of the Bible, whether popular or not."[48]

Many egalitarians were greatly troubled by Dobson's statement. In the Spring 2000 issue of the egalitarian newsletter *Mutuality,* there was an article by Kim Pettit, "Why I Disagree with Dobson and the SBC." In the article she objected that "endorsement of the SBC statement by an increasing number of Christian organizations means dissenters are excluded as this becomes a confessional issue."[49] Personally, I do not think that the SBC statement or others like it will mean that people who hold another view will be excluded from fellowship in the church. But I do think it means that people who hold an egalitarian view will be excluded from many teaching and governing positions within the denomination. Because I think that the egalitarian view is both harmful and contrary to Scripture, I think this is an appropriate result, and I think it is the one intended by those who added this statement to the "Baptist Faith and Message."

People who are right in the middle of turning points in history do not always realize it. I believe that today we are right in the middle of a turning point in the history of the church. Organizations right now are deciding these issues. They are making commitments and establishing those commitments in their policies. Some organizations are affirming biblical principles, as the Southern Baptists did. Others are establishing egalitarian principles as part of their policies, as Willow Creek Community Church has done.[50] There is a sifting, a sorting, a dividing going on within the evangelical world, and I believe that institutions that adopt an egalitarian position on this issue will drift farther and farther from faithfulness to the Bible on other issues as well.

What is "the way forward" regarding biblical manhood and womanhood? I believe the way forward is to add a clear statement to the governing document of your church, your denomination, or your parachurch organization.

Why should we do this? First, because it affects so much. As Christians, we can differ over issues of the Tribulation or the Millennium and still live largely the same way in our daily lives. But differences over this issue affect people's lives and result in "increasingly destructive consequences in our families, our churches, and the culture at large," to use the words of the Danvers Statement (Affirmation 10). Where biblical patterns are not followed, husbands and wives have no clear guidance on how to act within their marriages, and there is increasing stress that brings harmful and even destructive consequences to families.

The second reason I believe that organizations should add statements to their governing documents is that egalitarians have run out of new exegetical arguments, and they simply are not winning the arguments on the basis of the biblical text. As a result, it seems that their books increasingly deal not with detailed analysis of the words and sentences of Scripture but with broad generalizations about Scripture, then with arguments from experience or arguments from philosophical concepts such as "fairness," or from the supposed negative results of a complementarian position (such as spousal abuse, which they wrongly attribute to our position, but which we strongly oppose and condemn as well).[51] But it seems to me, and increasingly it seems to many others, that the egalitarian position has simply lost the arguments based on the meaning of the biblical text, and there are no more arguments to be made.

A third reason why I think organizations should add a statement on biblical manhood and womanhood to their governing documents is that I believe this is a "watershed issue." Many years ago Francis Schaeffer called the doctrine of biblical inerrancy a "watershed issue" because the position that people took regarding inerrancy determined where their teachings would lead in succeeding years. Schaeffer said that the first people who make a mistake on a watershed issue do so with only a very small step, and in all other areas of life they are godly and orthodox. And this was the case with a number of scholars who denied inerrancy in principle but did not change their beliefs on much of anything else. However, the next generation of leaders and scholars who come after them take the error much further. They see the implications of the change and they are consistent in working it out with regard to other matters of doctrine and practice, and thus they fall into greater and greater deviation from the teachings of the Bible.

I believe it is the same with this issue today. This controversy is the key to deeper issues and deeper commitments that touch every part of life. Though many egalitarians today do not adopt the other implications of their view (see discussion under "Key Issue 6," below), their followers will, and the next generation of leaders will go much farther in the denial of the truths of Scripture or their failure to be subject to Scripture in other parts of life. I said earlier that I believe one reason God has allowed this controversy into the church is so that we can correct wrongful male chauvinism in our churches and families. Now I need to say that I think there is another reason God has allowed this controversy into the church, and that is to test our hearts. Will we be faithful to Him and obey His Word or not?

In the Old Testament, God allowed false prophets to come among the people, but He had told them, "you shall not listen to the words of that prophet or to that dreamer of dreams; for the LORD your God is testing you, to know whether you love the LORD your God with all your heart and with all your soul" (Deut. 13:3). Now I am certainly not saying that egalitarians are the same as those in Old Testament times who advocated serving other gods, for egalitarians within evangelicalism do worship Jesus Christ as their Savior. But I am saying that there is a principle of God's actions in history in which He allows various kinds of false teaching to exist in the church, probably in every generation, and by these false teachings God tests His people, to see whether they will be faithful to His Word. In this generation, I believe that one of those tests is whether we will be faithful to God in the teaching of His Word on matters of manhood and womanhood.

A similar idea is found in 1 Corinthians 11:19: "for there must be factions among you, in order that those who are genuine among you may be recognized." When divisions and controversies arise in the church, people who make the right choices about the division eventually become "recognized," or are made "evident" (NASB). Others make wrong choices and thereby disqualify themselves from leadership. Charles Hodge wrote about this verse, "By the prevalence of disorders and other evils in the church, God puts his people to the test. They are tried as gold in the furnace, and their genuineness is made to appear."[52] Today, by the controversy over manhood and womanhood, I believe that God is testing all of His people, all of His churches. The egalitarian alternative would be so easy to adopt in today's culture, and it can appear on the surface to make so little difference. But will we remain faithful to the Word of God?

KEY ISSUE 6: THIS CONTROVERSY IS MUCH BIGGER THAN WE REALIZE, BECAUSE IT TOUCHES ALL OF LIFE

I also believe that the question of biblical manhood and womanhood is the focal point in a tremendous battle of worldviews. In that battle, biblical Christianity is being attacked simultaneously by two opponents who have great power over the dominant ideas in the cultures of the world. Opponent 1, on the left, may be called "No Differences," and its slogan would be, "All is one." Opponent 2, on the right, may be called "No Equality," and its slogan would be, "Might Makes Right."[53]

The chart on the following pages shows how a biblical view of men and women ("the complementarian middle") stands in contrast to the opponent "No Differences" on the far left and the opponent "No Equality" on the far right. For example, a biblical view of God includes equality and differences and unity. God is a Trinity where the Father, Son, and Holy Spirit have equal value and different roles, and they have absolute unity in the one being of God.

	THE EFFEMINATE LEFT — NO DIFFERENCES "All is one"	EGALITARIANISM — Removing or denying many differences between men & women	THE COMPLEMENTARIAN MIDDLE — EQUALITY and DIFFERENCES and UNITY — Emphasizing *both* equality and differences between men & women		MALE DOMINANCE — Over-emphasizing the differences between men and women	THE VIOLENT RIGHT — NO EQUALITY "Might makes right"
God	God = creation; God as Mother; Sophia worship; New Age worship	Mutual submission in the Trinity (F ↔ S ↔ HS)	God as Trinity (F → S, HS)	Father, Son, Holy Spirit: equal value, different roles	Arianism (Son and Holy Spirit not fully God) (F, S, HS)	God as one person, not a Trinity, not three persons. Harsh, unloving warrior-God (Allah)
Man / Woman	Emasculation of men; Defeminization of women	No gender-based role differences in marriage (no "Mars-Venus" differences)	(H → W)	Husband, wife equal value, different roles	Men are better than women; Excessive competitiveness to show women as inferior	Men as brutes; Women as objects; Dehumanization of women
Marriage	Same-sex "marriages" approved	"Mutual submission" Often: husband as "wimp," wife as "usurper"	Husband: loving, humble headship; Wife: intelligent, joyful submission to husband		Husband as harsh, selfish, "dictator"; Wife as "doormat"	Polygamy, harems, female infanticide
Children	Children murdered: abortion supported by women who reject feminine roles	Children raised with too little discipline, little respect for authority	Children loved, cared for, valued; Children raised with discipline and love		Children raised with harsh discipline, little love or compassion	Children murdered: abortion supported by men who reject masculine responsibility for family
Family Responsibilities	No family—just "society"	All responsibilities shared equally between husband and wife, or divided according to gifts and interests	Husband: responsible to lead, provide for, protect; Wife: responsible to help husband by managing household and nurturing children		Wives forbidden to have own job outside home, or to vote or own property, etc.	Men have all power, women and children are to serve them
Sex	Homosexuality; Lesbianism	Men become un-masculine, unattractive to women; Women become un-feminine, unattractive to men	Monogamous, equally fulfilling intercourse as deepest expression of a great "mystery": equality *and* differences *and* unity!		Pornography; Lust; Adultery	Violence against women; Rape
	Violent opposition to God's plan for sex as only between man and woman	Ambivalence toward sex	Delight in God's plan for sexual expression restrained by bonds of lifelong marriage		Excessive attention to sex	Violent opposition to God's plan for sex as only within marriage

	Temptation: unlimited same-sex sexual activity	Moving "contrary to nature" (Rom. 1:26)	Natural desires fulfilled — Men and women have deep sense of acting as God made them to act	Moving in exaggeration and distortion of nature	Temptation: unlimited unequal sexual activity
Natural Desires					
Religion	Feminized religion in churches Pantheism	No governing or teaching roles in church reserved for men	Some governing and teaching roles in church restricted to men	All ministry done by men; women's gifts squelched; Crusades	Militant forms of Islam Religion advanced by violence
Authority	Hatred of authority	Suspicion of authority	Authority exercised within boundaries	Over-use of authority	Abuse of authority
Sports	No competition "everybody wins"	Anti-competition	Competition with fairness and rules Winners honored, losers respected	Excessive competition Losers humiliated	Violent harm to opponents Gladiators fight to death WWF wrestling
Crime	No respect for authority, rampant crime, especially by frustrated, angry men	Criminal seen as victim to be helped, not punished; punishment long delayed	Punishment is speedy, fair; aims at justice plus restoration of criminal	Repressive government, little freedom, debtors' prisons	Excessive punishment, dehumanization of criminals (cut off hand of thief); little crime, but no freedom
Property	No private property; all possessions equalized	No one is allowed to be very rich; large-scale dependence on welfare state and government	Laws protect private property *and* care for poor; more work and skill earns more wealth; equal opportunity for all	Women cannot own property	Slavery; dehumanization of the poor and weak; all property in hands of few
Education	All-male schools prohibited by law; prohibitions against educating boys and girls separately	Systematic pressure to make boys and girls do equally well in all subjects	Boys and girls both educated, but different preferences, abilities, and sense of calling respected	Boys given preferential treatment in schools	Girls not allowed to be educated

Please note: This chart contains many generalizations and is only meant to show broad tendencies. Most people and many religious systems hold mixed views and have inconsistencies in thinking. Moreover, conscience, social pressure, and the Bible often restrain people from adopting all aspects of non-biblical views. Therefore this chart certainly *does not* imply that every person or religious system within each column holds to everything in that column. *This chart may be duplicated for teaching purposes without charge.*

The Left Column: No Differences. On the far left, the differences in the persons of God are abolished and the differences between God and the creation are abolished because "all is one." God then is viewed as equal to the creation, and people will worship the earth or parts of the earth as God (or as our "Mother"). Much New Age worship takes this form, as does much Eastern religion where the goal is to seek unity with the universe. When we follow the "no differences" theme into the area of manhood and womanhood, the attempt to obliterate differences leads to the emasculation of men and the defeminization of women. Men become more like women and women become more like men, because "all is one."

Within marriage, if there are no differences, then same-sex "marriages" would be approved. Women who reject feminine roles will support abortion. Since there are no distinct roles for a child's father and mother within the family, there's really no longer any need to have children raised by the family; rather, "society" can take care of raising children. Within the realm of sexuality, homosexuality and lesbianism will be approved. The chart then details how the "no differences," "all should be one" theme will work out in feminized religion within churches, in hatred of authority (for if someone has more authority, then all is not one), in a loss of competitiveness in sports (for if we have "winners" and "losers," then all is not one), in no respect for authority in the civil realm (with an increase in rampant crime), in attempts to abolish private property and to equalize possessions (for no one can be different, but all should be one), and in attempts to prohibit all-male schools or to prohibit educating boys and girls separately. These are the tendencies that follow once we adopt the conviction that "all is one." If there are no differences of persons in the being of God, there should be no differences between men and women either.

The Egalitarian Column: Remove Many Differences. What concerns me about the egalitarian viewpoint within evangelicalism is that it tends toward removing or denying many differences between men and women. Egalitarians have begun to deny eternal personal distinctions among the Father, Son, and Holy Spirit, and argue rather for "mutual submission" within the Trinity. They deny that there are any gender-based role differences in marriage.[54] Within marriage, an egalitarian view tends toward abolishing differences and advocates "mutual submission," which often results in the husband acting as a "wimp" and the wife as a "usurper." Because there is a deep-seated opposition to most authority, the drive toward "sameness" will often result in children being raised with too little discipline and too little respect for authority. Within the family, there will be a tendency toward sharing all responsibilities equally between husband and wife, or to dividing responsibilities according to gifts and interests, not according to roles as specified by Scripture. Within the realm of human sexuality, tendencies to deny the differences between men and women will often result in men becoming unmasculine and unattractive to women and women becoming unfeminine and unattractive to men. There will often be ambivalence toward sex.

The chart goes on to show how, within the realm of religion, the egalitarian view tends toward removing or denying many differences between men and women, and supports the idea that no governing or teaching roles within the church should be reserved for men. Within sports, this view would tend to be opposed to competition and think of it as evil rather than good. With respect to crime, the criminal would be seen as a victim to be helped and not punished, and punishment would be long delayed. As far as private property is concerned, because there are tendencies to abolish differences, no one would be allowed to be very rich, and there would be large-scale dependence on the welfare state and on government. Within education, there would be systematic pressure to make boys and girls participate equally and do equally well in all subjects and all activities, forcibly attempting to eradicate any patterns of natural preferences and aptitudes for some kinds of activities by boys and some kinds by girls. All of this would tend toward a denial of differences between men and women.

The Far Right Column: No Equality. But there are opposite errors as well. The opponent on the far right side of the chart is "No Equality," and the dominant idea from this perspective is that there is no equality between persons who are different. Rather, the stronger person is more valuable, and the weaker person is devalued, for "might makes right." In this view, God is not viewed as a Trinity but as one person who is all-powerful. Often God can be viewed as a harsh, unloving warrior God, as in a common Islamic view of Allah, as well as in a number of tribal religions. In this perspective, since "might makes right" and the weaker person is viewed as inferior, the relationships between men and women get distorted. Men begin to act as brutes and they treat women as objects. This view dehumanizes women. Whereas the "No Differences" error most significantly results in the destruction of men, the "No Equality" error most significantly results in the destruction of women.

Within marriage, the idea that there is no equality in value between men and women will lead to polygamy and harems. There is no concern to value women equally, for "might makes right" and men are stronger. This view also leads to female infanticide, because people prefer to have boys. With regard to children, men who reject masculine responsibility to care for their families will support and encourage abortion. Within the family, if there is no equality in value before God, men will have all the power, and women and children will exist simply to serve them. Within the realm of sexuality, the "No Equality" error results in rape and other violence against women.

The chart also shows how this viewpoint works out in religion, where religion is advanced by violence and force (as in militant forms of Islam). The view that there need be no equality of value between persons results in the destruction of people who have less power or less authority, so authority is abused as a result. Within sports, this view will lead to violent harm to opponents, and even to gladiators fighting to the death. (The increasing popularity of violent and harmful wrestling programs on television is a manifestation of this tendency.) As far as criminal justice, this view will lead to excessive punishment and dehumanization of criminals (such as cutting off the hand of a thief, or putting people to death for expressing different religious beliefs). There will often be little outward crime in the society, but on the other hand there will be little freedom. As far as private property is concerned, there will be slavery and dehumanization of the poor and weak, while all property is held in the hands of a few who are very powerful. In education, the "No Equality" viewpoint would result in girls not being allowed to obtain an education.

The Male Dominance Column: Overemphasizing the Differences and Neglecting Equality. There have been disturbing tendencies leading in the direction of "No Equality" and advocating that "might makes right" whenever a "Male Dominance" view has found expression within the church or society. This view overemphasizes the differences between men and women and does not treat women as having equal value to men, nor would it treat those under authority as having equal value to those who have authority. With respect to a view of God, this view, which might be called the "domineering right," would be parallel to Arianism (the view that the Son and Holy Spirit are not fully God in the sense that the Father is God, but are lesser, created beings). In relationships between men and women, this viewpoint would foster an attitude that men are better than women, and it would result in excessive competitiveness in which a man feels he always has to win in any sport or in any argument with a woman, in order to show that women are inferior.

Within marriage, this "Male Dominance" error would result in a husband being harsh and selfish and acting as a "dictator" or a "tyrant," and the wife acting as a "doormat." Because there is too great an emphasis on authority, this view would tend toward a system where children are raised with harsh discipline but with little love or compassion. As far as family responsibilities, wives would be forbidden to have their own jobs outside the home, or to vote, or to own property, for there is no thought of treating them as equal.

Within the realm of sexuality, a "Male Dominance" view would result in pornography and adultery and hearts filled with lust. There would be excessive attention given to sex, with men focusing on their own sexual desires. People may wonder why involvement with pornography often leads to violence against women, but this chart makes the connection clear: Pornography looks at women as objects for sexual gratification, not as persons equal in God's sight; violence against women just takes that idea one step further and begins to treat them as objects and as unworthy of dignity and respect.

The chart goes on to point out how "Male Dominance" would work out in a religious system where all ministry is done by men and women's gifts are suppressed and squelched. This view would also lead to things like the Crusades, the mistaken military expeditions in the eleventh, twelfth, and thirteenth centuries that were carried out to regain control of the Holy Land from the Muslims by force. Within sports, there would be excessive competition and losers would be humiliated. Regarding crime, there would be a repressive government with little freedom, and things like debtors' prisons would dehumanize the poor. Women would not be permitted to own property, and boys would be given preferential treatment in schools.

The Complementarian Middle Column: Equality and Differences and Unity All Maintained. In contrast to these errors in both directions, the biblical picture is one that emphasizes *equality* and *differences* and *unity* at the same time. Parallel to the equality and differences among the members of the Trinity, in a complementarian view men and women are equal in value but have different roles. Within marriage, a husband will manifest loving, humble headship, and a wife will manifest intelligent, joyful submission to her husband's leadership. Children will be loved and cared for and valued, and they will be raised with both discipline and love. Children will respect the authority of their parents, but their parents will respect the dignity of children as having equal value because they are persons created in the image of God. Within the family, there will be a division of responsibilities in which the husband is primarily responsible to lead, provide for, and protect his family. The wife, on the other hand, will be primarily responsible to help her husband by managing the household and nurturing the children, though both husband and wife will often participate willingly in helping the other person with his or her area of primary responsibility.

In the realm of sexuality, a complementarian view will result in monogamous, lifelong marriage and in equally fulfilling experiences of sex as the deepest expression of a great "mystery" created by God:

We are equal, and we are different, and we are one! There will be a delight in God's plan for sexual expression, but it will be restrained by the bonds of lifelong faithfulness to one's marriage partner. Men and women will have then a deep sense of acting in the way that God created them to act in all these areas.

The chart goes on to explain how a complementarian view works out in religion, where some governing and teaching roles in the church are restricted to men, but women's gifts are also honored and used fully in the ministries of the church. In all areas of life, authority will be exercised within boundaries so that the person under authority is treated with respect and dignity, and treated as someone who shares equally in the image of God. Within sports, there will be an appreciation for competition that will include fairness and rules, and winners will be honored while losers are respected. Equality. Differences. Unity.

As far as crime, punishment will be speedy and fair and will aim at satisfying justice as well as restoring the criminal. Laws will protect private property but will also reflect care for the poor. People will be rewarded according to their work and skill, and there will be a desire to have equal opportunity for all in the economic realm. Within education, both boys and girls will be educated but different preferences and abilities and senses of calling among boys and girls will be respected, and no quotas will be imposed to force an artificial equality in number of participants in every activity where that would not have resulted from allowing boys and girls to choose activities freely of their own accord. Equality. Differences. Unity.

I realize, of course, that any chart like this has generalizations and that people may not hold all the viewpoints represented within a particular column. Nevertheless, I think the chart has significant value in showing that we will continually face two opposing challenges in trying to uphold a biblical viewpoint of manhood and womanhood. People on the domineering right will continue to think of us as weak and yielding too much to the demands of feminism. People on the egalitarian left will continue to see us as harsh and overemphasizing the differences between men and women. But we must steadfastly and patiently hold to the middle, with the help of God.

By now it should be plain why I say that this controversy is bigger than we realize. The struggle to uphold equality *and* differences *and* unity between men and women has implications for all areas of life. Moreover, strong spiritual forces invisibly war against us in this whole controversy. I am not now focusing on the egalitarian left or the domineering right, but on the far left column and the far right column, the effeminate left and the violent right. I do not think that we can look at those two columns for long without realizing that behind the attempt to abolish all differences and make everything "one," and behind the attempt to destroy those who are weaker and make the stronger always "right," there is deep spiritual evil. At both extremes, the hand of the Enemy seeks to destroy God's idea of sex, of marriage, and of manhood and womanhood. We see the hand of the Enemy seeking to destroy everything that glorifies God, especially the beauty of our sexual differences, which wonderfully reflect God's glory. The Enemy hates everything that God created as good, and hates everything that brings glory to God Himself.

So in the end, this whole controversy is really about God and how His character is reflected in the beauty and excellence of manhood and womanhood as He created it. Will we glorify God through manhood and womanhood lived according to His Word? Or will we deny His Word and give in to the pressures of modern culture? That is the choice we have to make.

NOTES

1. Unless otherwise indicated, all Scripture quotations in this chapter are from the Revised Standard Version of the Bible. Italics in Scripture quotations have been added by the author for emphasis.

2. For further discussion, see Wayne Grudem, *Systematic Theology: An Introduction to Biblical Doctrine* (Leicester, England: InterVarsity; and Grand Rapids, Mich.: Zondervan, 1994), 442-450.

3. God created us so that our likeness to Him would be seen in our moral judgment and actions, in our spiritual life and ability to relate to God who is spirit, in our reasoning ability, our use of language, our awareness of the distant past and future, our creativity, the complexity and variety of our emotions, the

depth of our interpersonal relationships, our equality and differences in marriage and other interpersonal relationships, our rule over the rest of creation, and in other ways. All of these aspects are distorted by sin and manifest themselves in ways that are *unlike* God and are displeasing to Him, but all of these areas of our lives are also being progressively restored to greater God-likeness through the salvation that is ours in Christ, and they will be completely restored in us when Christ returns.

4. In 1 Corinthians 11:7 Paul says, "A man ought not to cover his head, since he is the image and glory of God; but woman is the glory of man." He is not denying here that woman was created in the image of God, for that is clearly affirmed in Genesis 1:27. Nor does he say that woman is the image of man. Rather, Paul is simply saying that *in the relationship between man and woman,* man in particular reflects something of the excellence of the God who created him, and woman *in that relationship* reflects something of the excellence of the man from whom she was created. Yet Paul goes on almost immediately to say that men and women are interdependent (1 Cor. 11:11-12), and that we could not exist without each other. He does not say in this passage that man is more in the image of God than woman is, nor should we derive any such idea from this passage.

5. A tragic example of male dominance was reported on the front page of *USA Today: International Edition* (Sept. 6, 1994): "No Girls Allowed: Abortion for sex selection raises moral questions" was the caption on a photo of a doctor performing an ultrasound on a pregnant woman in India. The cover story, "Asians' desire for boys leaves a deadly choice," reported that according to Dr. Datta Pai, a Bombay obstetrician, "99% of those found to be carrying female fetuses aborted their unborn children" (2A). The story explained that "modern technology, the strong cultural desire for boys and pressure to reduce population have joined forces in a deadly combination in India, China and much of Asia to produce a booming business in sex selection. . . . [T]he practice of aborting female fetuses appears common judging by emerging statistics that show lopsided sex ratios throughout Asia and into North Africa. Nor is the practice of sex selection limited to abortion. Female infanticide, the abandonment of baby girls, and the preferential feeding and health care of boys contribute greatly to the imbalanced ratios" (1A-2A). The story goes on to quote Harvard professor Amartya Sen as saying that there are now more than 100,000,000 women "missing" in the population of the world, including 44,000,000 fewer women in China and 37,000,000 fewer in India than should be alive according to normal sex ratios at birth (2A).

This is a tragedy of unspeakable proportions. In addition to the harm of these lost lives, we must think of the destructive consequences in the lives of those women who survive. From their earliest age they receive the message from their families, and indeed from their whole society, "Boys are better than girls," and "I wish you were a boy." The devastation on their own sense of self-worth must be immense. Yet all of this comes about as a result of a failure to realize that men and women, boys and girls, have equal value in God's sight and should have equal value in our sight as well. The first chapter of the Bible corrects this practice, and corrects any lurking sense in our own hearts that boys are more valuable than girls, when it says we are both created in the image of God.

6. The fact that both men and women are baptized stands in contrast to the Old Testament, where the outward sign of inclusion in the community of God's people was circumcision: circumcision by its nature was only administered to men. By contrast, in the New Testament church both men and women are baptized. In this way, every baptism should remind us of our equality in the image of God.

7. I realize that there is an opposite mistake, in which the husband "listens" so much and the wife has so great a "voice" that in effect the wife becomes the governing partner in the relationship. I am not advocating that mistake either, and in what follows I will argue for the necessity of a male leadership role in decision making within marriage.

8. Policy statement announced and distributed to Campus Crusade staff members at a biannual staff conference, July 28, 1999, at Moby Arena, Colorado State University, Fort Collins, Colorado. The statement was reported in a Religion News Service dispatch July 30, 1999, a Baptist Press story by Art Toalston on July 29, 1999 (www.baptistpress.com), and an article in *World* magazine September 11, 1999 (32); it was also quoted in full in James Dobson's monthly newsletter *Family News from Dr. James Dobson* (September 1999), 1-2.

9. Throughout this chapter, I use the word "egalitarian" to refer to those within the evangelical world who say that no differences in the roles of men and women should be based on their gender alone. In particular, "egalitarians" deny that there is any unique male leadership role in marriage or in the church. Sometimes I use the phrase "evangelical feminists" to mean the same thing as "egalitarians."

10. The Danvers Statement was prepared by several evangelical leaders at a Council on Biblical Manhood and Womanhood meeting in Danvers, Massachusetts, in December 1987. It was first published in final form by the CBMW in Wheaton, Illinois, in November 1988. See the appendix for the full text of this statement.

11. The entire statement in the form adopted by Campus Crusade for Christ is available at www.baptistpress.com, in the archives for July 29, 1999.

12. The entire statement is available from the website of Christians for Biblical Equality, www.cbeinternational.org. I should add that the CBE statement regularly portrays a non-egalitarian position in pejorative language such as "the rulership of Adam over Eve," and fails to even mention a third alternative, namely, loving, humble headship. (For a discussion of repeated ambiguities in the CBE statement, see John Piper and Wayne Grudem, "Charity, Clarity, and Hope," in Piper and Grudem, eds., *Recovering Biblical Manhood and Womanhood* [Wheaton, Ill.: Crossway, 1991], 403-422.)

13. Bruce Ware adds yet another indication related to this temporal priority in creation, namely, that woman was created "from" or "out of" man. See his discussion in "Male and Female Complementarity and the Image of God,"

chapter 2 of *Biblical Foundations for Manhood and Womanhood* (Wheaton, Ill.: Crossway, 2002). Although I have not listed it separately here, it could be counted as an eleventh indication along with the ten I list.

14. See Gilbert Bilezikian, *Beyond Sex Roles,* 2nd edn. (Grand Rapids, Mich.: Baker, 1990), 259, where he says, "No mention of 'giving a name' is made in reference to the woman in verse 23." He also says, "The contrast between Genesis 2:23 and 3:20 bears out the fact that there was no act of naming in the first instance. When Eve actually receives her *name,* the text uses that very word, 'The man called his wife's *name* Eve'" (261). Bilezikian apparently thinks that where the word "name" (the Hebrew noun *shēm*) is not used, no act of naming occurs. But he takes no account of the fact that the noun *shēm* is not used in Genesis 1:5, 8, or 10 either, where God names the "Day" and the "Night," and "Heaven" and "Earth" and "Seas." The idea of naming can be indicated by the verb *qārā'* without the noun "name" being used.

15. Similarly, because God is having Adam examine and name the entire animal kingdom, it is likely that Adam gave names to one representative of each broad category or type of animal in Genesis 2:19-20 (such as "dog," "cat," "deer," or "lion," to use English equivalents). We hardly expect that he would have given individual, personal names (such as "Rover," or "Tabby," or "Bambi," or "Leo"), because those names would not have applied to others of the same kind. This distinction is missed by Gilbert Bilezikian (*Beyond Sex Roles,* 259-261) when he objects that Adam did not name Eve until Genesis 3:20, after the Fall. He did give her a specific personal name ("Eve") after the Fall, but he also gave her the general category name "Woman" before the Fall.

16. There are actually more than thirteen instances where the Hebrew word *'ādām* referred to a male human being, because prior to the creation of Eve there are twelve additional instances where references to "the man" spoke only of a male person whom God has created: see Genesis 2:5, 7 (twice), 8, 15, 16, 18, 19 (twice), 20 (twice), 21. If we add these instances, there are twenty-five examples of *'ādām* used to refer to a male human being prior to Genesis 5:2. The male connotations of the word could not have been missed by the original readers.

17. Raymond C. Ortlund, Jr., "Male-Female Equality and Male Headship," in Piper and Grudem, eds., *Recovering Biblical Manhood and Womanhood,* 98.

18. It is interesting to notice that several gender-neutral Bible translations have changed the word "man," which was standard in earlier English translations. The word "humankind" is used in the New Revised Standard Version of Genesis 1:26-27. The New Living Translation uses the word "people," while the inclusive language edition of the New International Version uses the phrase "human beings." In Genesis 5:2, various gender-neutral substitutes replace the name "man": "humankind" (NRSV), "human" (NLT), or "human beings" (NIV-Inclusive Language Edition, CEV, NCV).

19. I am taking this analogy from Raymond C. Ortlund, Jr., in Piper and Grudem, eds., *Recovering Biblical Manhood and Womanhood,* 104.

20. This is the definition given in Francis Brown, S. R. Driver, and Charles A.

Briggs, *A Hebrew and English Lexicon of the Old Testament* (BDB) (Oxford: Clarendon, 1968), 617.

21. The ESV margin gives "against" as an alternative for *teshûqāh* + *'el* in Genesis 3:16 and 4:7. This seems to be the most accurate rendering. The preposition *'el* can take the meaning "against," as is clear from the next verse, Gen. 4:8, where "Cain rose up *against* (*'el*) his brother Abel, and killed him." *BDB* gives sense 4 for *'el* as: "Where the motion or direction implied appears from the context to be of a hostile character, *'el* = *against.*" They cite Gen. 4:8 and several other verses (40).

22. The only other occurrence of the word *teshûqāh* in the entire Hebrew Old Testament is found in Song of Solomon 7:10 (verse 11 in Hebrew), "I am my beloved's, and his *desire* is for me." There the word does not indicate a hostile or aggressive desire, but the man's sexual desire for his wife.

I had previously argued that a positive kind of "desire to conquer" could be understood in Song of Solomon 7:10, whereby it indicated the man's desire to have a kind of influence over his beloved that is appropriate to initiating and consummating the sexual relationship, an influence such that she would receive and yield to his amorous advances. This sense would be represented by the paraphrase, "His desire is to have me yield to him."

However, I am now inclined to think that the word *teshûqāh* itself does not signify anything so specific as "desire to conquer" but rather something more general such as "urge, impulse." (The word takes that sense in Mishnaic Hebrew, as indicated by David Talley in the following footnote.) In that case, Genesis 3:16 and 4:7 have the sense "desire, urge, impulse *against*" and Song of Solomon 7:10 has the sense "desire, urge, impulse *for.*" This seems to me to fit better with the context of Song of Solomon 7:10.

The difference in meaning may also be signaled by the different constructions. The Genesis and Song of Solomon examples are not exactly parallel linguistically, because a different preposition follows the verb in Song of Solomon and therefore the sense may be somewhat different. In Song of Solomon 7:11, *teshûqāh* is followed by *'al,* but it is followed by *'el* in Genesis 3:16 and 4:7.

(The preposition *'al* is misprinted as *'el* in Song of Solomon 7:11 as cited in *BDB,* 1003. *BDB* apparently does this because they follow the *Biblia Hebraica Stuttgartensia* editors [1334] who in the margin suggest changing the Hebrew text to *'el,* but this is mere conjecture with no manuscript support. The LXX confirms the difference, translating with *pros* for *'el* in Gen. 3:16 and 4:7 but with *epi* for *'al* in Song of Solomon 7:11, which is what we would expect with a very literal translation.)

In any case, while the sense in Song of Solomon 7:10 (11) is different, both the context and the construction are different, and this example is removed in time and authorship from Genesis 3:16 and must be given lower importance in understanding the meaning of the word in Genesis. Surely the sense cannot be "sexual desire" in Gen. 4:7, and it seems very unlikely in the context of Gen. 3:16 as well.

23. The understanding of Genesis 3:16 as a hostile desire, or even a desire to rule

over, has gained significant support among Old Testament commentators. It was first suggested by Susan T. Foh, "What Is the Woman's Desire?" *Westminster Theological Journal* 37 (1975), 376-383. David Talley says the word is attested in Samaritan and Mishnaic Hebrew "with the meaning urge, craving, impulse," and says of Foh, "Her contention that the desire is a contention for leadership, a negative usage, seems probable for Gen. 3:16" (Talley, in W. A. VanGemeren, ed., *New International Dictionary of Old Testament Theology and Exegesis,* vol. 4 [Grand Rapids, Mich.: Zondervan, 1997], 341, with reference to various commentators).

24. There was a foreshadowing of these New Testament commands in the godly marriages found in the Old Testament and in the honor given to women in passages such as Ruth, Esther, and Proverbs 31. But in the unfolding of God's plan of redemption, He waited until the New Testament to give the full and explicit directions for the marriage relationship that we find in Ephesians 5, Colossians 3, and 1 Peter 3.

25. This does not mean that I make every decision in our family. There are large areas of responsibility in which Margaret makes hundreds of decisions that I often do not even know about and certainly do not try to micromanage or second-guess (for example, with respect to household budgets for food, clothing, gifts, or other matters, which she controls; and with respect to the decoration and appearance of our home; and with respect to large sections of time each week when she has her own activities and I have mine). I think there remains some element of male headship in those areas in principle, but in practice she decides these things independently, as I do with respect to allocations of time and money related to my work. But when I say "the responsibility to make the decision rests with me," I am talking about the hundreds of other decisions that directly affect both of us, especially concerning activities in which we are both involved.

26. For further discussion, see John Piper, "A Vision of Biblical Complementarity: Manhood and Womanhood Defined According to the Bible," in Piper and Grudem, eds., *Recovering Biblical Manhood and Womanhood,* 31-59. See also Dorothy Patterson, "The High Calling of Wife and Mother in Biblical Perspective," 364-377, in the same volume.

27. On Galatians 3:28, see Richard W. Hove, *Equality in Christ? Galatians 3:28 and the Gender Dispute* (Wheaton, Ill.: Crossway, 1999). On Ephesians 5:21, see Wayne Grudem, "The Myth of 'Mutual Submission.'" *CBMW News* 1/4 (October 1996), 1-4. On the meaning of *kephalē,* see Wayne Grudem, "The Meaning of κεφαλή, ('head'): An Analysis of New Evidence, Real and Alleged," *Journal of the Evangelical Theological Society (JETS)* 44/1 (March 2001), 25-65.

I have also edited a book (a companion volume to this present volume) that contains more detailed essays on some of these questions: see Wayne Grudem, ed., *Biblical Foundations for Manhood and Womanhood* (Wheaton, Ill.: Crossway, 2002), especially the essays by Richard W. Hove, "Does Galatians 3:28 Negate Gender-Specific Roles?"; Wayne Grudem, "The Myth of Mutual Submission as an Interpretation of Ephesians 5:21"; Daniel Doriani, "The Historical

Novelty of Egalitarian Interpretations of Ephesians 5:21-22"; and Wayne Grudem, "The Meaning of 'Head' (*Kephalē*) in 1 Corinthians 11:3 and Ephesians 5:23," which is a reprint with only slight modifications of my article, "The Meaning of κεφαλή, ('head'): An Analysis of New Evidence, Real and Alleged," *JETS* 44/1 (March 2001), 25-65.

My two earlier studies on the meaning of *kephalē* were "The Meaning of *kephalē* ('Head'): A Response to Recent Studies," *Trinity Journal* 11NS (Spring 1990), 3-72; reprinted in Piper and Grudem, eds., *Recovering Biblical Manhood and Womanhood,* 425-68; and "Does *kephalē* ('head') Mean 'Source' or 'Authority Over' in Greek Literature? A Survey of 2,336 Examples," appendix in *The Role Relationship of Men and Women* (rev. edn.), George W. Knight III, (Chicago: Moody, 1985), 49-80, also printed in *Trinity Journal* 6 NS (Spring 1985), 38-59.

28. See Hove, *Equality in Christ?* and his essay "Galatians 3:28," mentioned in the note above.

29. Hove (*Equality in Christ*) ran forty-five computer searches on Greek literature near the time of the New Testament. He reports finding sixteen examples of Greek expressions from the New Testament and other ancient literature that use the verb "to be" (*eimi*) plus the number "one" (Greek *heis/ mia/ hen*) and finds that the expression is never used to indicate unity among things that are identical but always among things that are different and have different functions, but that also share something in common that gives them a kind of unity (72-76).

30. In fact, egalitarians have a journal called *Mutuality,* published by the organization Christians for Biblical Equality.

31. When the Southern Baptist Convention was debating its statement on marriage and the family, I am told that there was a motion from the floor to add "mutual submission" to the statement. A member of the drafting committee spoke against the motion and explained how egalitarians have used it to deny any sense of male authority within marriage. The motion was defeated, and appropriately so. If "mutual submission" had been added to the Southern Baptist statement, in effect it would have torpedoed the whole statement, because it would have watered it down so much that people from almost any position could have signed it, and it would have affirmed no unique male authority within marriage. (These events were reported to me by friends who were present when the statement was being debated on the floor of the Southern Baptist Convention in the summer of 1998.)

32. See Doriani, "Historical Novelty," in *Biblical Foundations for Manhood and Womanhood.*

33. The Greek text has the adjective *idios,* meaning "your own."

34. First Corinthians 16:15-16 should also be placed in this category, because it seems from 1 Clement 42:4, a letter written from Clement of Rome to the church of Corinth in 95 A.D., that the elders in the church at Corinth came from the household of Stephanas (note the allusion to 1 Cor. 16:15 with the expression "first converts" [Greek *aparchē*]). Therefore, when Paul tells the

Corinthians to be "subject to" the household of Stephanas, he is telling them to be subject to those who were elders in Corinth.

35. Some people have sent me e-mails saying that the example I am asking for is found in Ephesians 5:21, where *hypotassō* "obviously" means mutual submission and therefore it can't mean to be subject to an authority. Their claim simply shows that they have not understood the question. We are not free, in interpreting the Bible, to give a word any meaning we might think "fits." Words have established ranges of meanings that were familiar to native speakers of Greek in the ancient world and that allowed them to understand one another (that is how all language functions—speakers and hearers have in their minds "shared meanings" of thousands of words). Those established meanings are listed in dictionaries (or "lexicons") of ancient Greek. I am simply asking for some evidence showing that "be considerate of" with no idea of submission to an authority was an established, shared meaning of *hypotassō* in the ancient world. No one has produced any such evidence.

To claim (as these e-mail writers have claimed to me) that *hypotassō* means something in Ephesians 5:21 that it nowhere meant at any other time or place in history would require (1) that Paul used a word with a new, secret meaning that Greek-speaking people had never known before, and (2) that Paul expected that all the Christians in all the churches to which the letter to the Ephesians went would know this new, secret meaning and understand what he meant, and (3) that they would know that he did not mean by *hypotassō* what all Greek speakers everywhere had previously meant when they used it in conversation, and even what Paul himself meant by it in all his other writings, and (4) that all subsequent writers in over 1,900 years of church history have failed to discern this non-authoritative meaning for *hypotassō*, and (5) that the meaning is now suddenly so "obvious" from the context that everyone should see it.

People may believe such a position if they wish, but it will be for reasons other than evidence or facts.

36. It is interesting that the King James Version showed an understanding of the sense of *allēlous* in this passage. It translated the verse, "submitting yourselves *one to another* in the fear of God." In fact, when *allēlous* takes the sense "some to others," the King James Version often signaled that by phrases such as "one to another."

37. I realize that a few egalitarians claim that Paul's teaching only applied to his time in history and is not applicable to us today. This particular position is not affected by disputes over the meaning of the word "head" but it is very difficult to sustain in light of the parallel with Christ and the church, and in light of Paul's tying it to the statements about marriage before there was sin in the world (Eph. 5:31-32, quoting Gen. 2:24).

38. For details, see Wayne Grudem, "Does *Kephalē* ('Head') Mean 'Source' or 'Authority Over' in Greek Literature? A Survey of 2,336 Examples," *Trinity Journal* 6 NS (Spring 1985), 38-59. I published two further studies on *kephalē* in 1990 and 2001, which are cited in footnote 27 above.

39. In the 1950s, Bedale still argued for authority attaching to the meaning of the word, though he was the first to propose the sense "source" for this passage.

See Stephen Bedale, "The Meaning of *kephalē* in the Pauline Epistles," *Journal of Theological Studies* 5 (1954), 211-215.

40. Personal letter from P. G. W. Glare to Wayne Grudem, April 14, 1997. Quoted by permission. Italics added.

41. See my extended discussion of the meaning of *kephale* cited in footnote 27 above.

42. See Craig Keener's affirmation of an eternal subordination of the Son to the Father in, "Is Subordination Within the Trinity Really Heresy? A Study of John 5:18 in Context," *Trinity Journal* 20 NS (1999), 39-51.

43. For a fuller discussion of egalitarian tampering with the doctrine of the Trinity, see Bruce Ware, "Tampering with the Trinity: Does the Son Submit to His Father?" in Wayne Grudem, ed., *Biblical Foundations for Manhood and Womanhood* (Wheaton, Ill.: Crossway, 2002). The primary statements by Bilezikian and Grenz are found in Gilbert Bilezikian, "Hermeneutical Bungee-Jumping: Subordination in the Godhead," *JETS* 40/1 (March 1997) 57-68; and Stanley J. Grenz, "Theological Foundations for Male-Female Relationships," *JETS* 41/4 (December 1998), 615-630.

A survey of historical evidence showing affirmation of the eternal subordination of the Son to the authority of the Father is found in Stephen D. Kovach and Peter R. Schemm, Jr., "A Defense of the Doctrine of the Eternal Subordination of the Son," in *JETS* 42/3 (September 1999), 461-476. See also Wayne Grudem, *Systematic Theology* (Leicester, England: InterVarsity; and Grand Rapids, Mich.: Zondervan, 1994), 248-252.

44. See John Gray, *Men Are from Mars, Women Are from Venus* (New York: HarperCollins, 1992), and several other books written by Gray on a similar theme; see also Debra Tannen, *You Just Don't Understand: Women and Men in Conversation* (New York: Ballantine, 1990).

45. This is the text of the June 1998 addition to the Southern Baptist Convention's statement, "The Baptist Faith and Message":

XVIII. The Family

God has ordained the family as the foundational institution of human society. It is composed of persons related to one another by marriage, blood, or adoption.

Marriage is the uniting of one man and one woman in covenant commitment for a lifetime. It is God's unique gift to reveal the union between Christ and His church, and to provide for the man and the woman in marriage the framework for intimate companionship, the channel of sexual expression according to biblical standards, and the means for procreation of the human race.

The husband and wife are of equal worth before God, since both are created in God's image. The marriage relationship models the way God relates to His people. A husband is to love his wife as Christ loved the church. He has the God-given responsibility to provide for, to protect, and to lead his family. A wife is to submit herself graciously to the servant leadership of her husband even as the church willingly submits to the headship of Christ. She, being in the image of God as is her husband and thus equal to him, has the God-given responsibility to respect her husband and to serve as his helper in managing the household and nurturing the next generation.

Children, from the moment of conception, are a blessing and heritage from the Lord. Parents are to demonstrate to their children God's pattern for marriage. Parents are to teach their children spiritual and moral values and to lead them, through consistent lifestyle example and loving discipline, to make choices based on biblical truth. Children are to honor and obey their parents.

Genesis 1:26-28; 2:15-25; 3:1-20; Exodus 20:12; Deuteronomy 6:4-9; Joshua 24:15; 1 Samuel 1:26-28; Psalms 51:5; 78:1-8; 127; 128; 139:13-16; Proverbs 1:8; 5:15-20; 6:20-22; 12:4; 13:24; 14:1; 17:6; 18:22; 22:6,15; 23:13-14; 24:3; 29:15,17; 31:10-31; Ecclesiastes 4:9-12; 9:9; Malachi 2:14-16; Matthew 5:31-32; 18:2-5; 19:3-9; Mark 10:6-12; Romans 1:18-32; 1 Corinthians 7:1-16; Ephesians 5:21-33; 6:1-4; Colossians 3:18-21; 1 Timothy 5:8, 14; 2 Timothy 1:3-5; Titus 2:3-5; Hebrews 13:4; 1 Peter 3:1-7.

In addition, in June 2000, the SBC also added the following sentence to Article VI, "The Church": "While both men and women are gifted for service in the church, the office of pastor is limited to men as qualified by Scripture."

46. "Southern Baptists . . . you are right! We stand with you!" *USA Today,* August 26, 1998, 5D.

47. See above, under "Key Issues 1 and 2," for a discussion of the Campus Crusade policy statement.

48. *Family News from Dr. James Dobson* (September 1999), 1-2.

49. Kim Pettit, "Why I Disagree with Dobson and the SBC," *Mutuality* (Spring 2000), 17.

50. See Wayne Grudem, "Willow Creek Enforces Egalitarianism: Policy Requires All Staff and New Members to Joyfully Affirm Egalitarian Views," in *CBMW News* 2/5 (December 1997), 1, 3-6.

51. I still regret, and still cannot understand, why the board of directors of Christians for Biblical Equality declined to issue a joint statement with the Council on Biblical Manhood and Womanhood on the issue of abuse. CBMW adopted the statement in November 1994, and has continued to distribute it widely through its literature and its website, www.cbmw.org. The letter from CBE in which they declined to issue a statement jointly with us can be found in *CBMW News* 1/1 (August 1995), 3, and is available at www.cbmw.org/journal/editions/1-1.pdf

52. Charles Hodge, *An Exposition of 1 and 2 Corinthians* (Wilmington, Del.: Sovereign Grace, 1972; first published 1857), 125.

53. The groundbreaking ideas of Peter Jones and Dan Heimbach, fellow members of the Council on Biblical Manhood and Womanhood, provided the fundamental concepts that led to the following material. I am grateful for their contributions, though the specific applications that follow are my own. See the

chapters by Jones and Heimbach in Wayne Grudem, ed., *Biblical Foundations for Manhood and Womanhood.*

54. There was an amusing but very revealing suggestion for a new title to the book, *Men Are from Mars, Women Are from Venus,* in the CBE publication *Mutuality:* In an imaginary conversation in a bookstore, the writer suggested that a better title for a book about men and women would be, *Men Are from Mars, Women Are from Venus, but Some Men Are from Venus and Some Women Are from Mars, and All of God's Children Have Both Mars and Venus Qualities Within Them, So Why Not Just Say that Men and Women Are from the Earth, and Let's Get About the Business of Developing the Unique God-given Mars/Venus Qualities that God Has Given All of Us for the Sake of the Kingdom* (article by Jim Banks in *Mutuality* [May 1998], 3). What was so revealing about this humorous suggestion was the way it showed that egalitarians seem to feel compelled to oppose any kinds of differences between men and women other than those that are purely physical.

II

MARRIAGE
GOD'S WAY

————∞∞∞————

3

THE SURPASSING GOAL: MARRIAGE LIVED FOR THE GLORY OF GOD

John Piper

—⟨∞⟩—

My topic for this chapter is "Marriage lived for the glory of God." The decisive word in that topic is the word "for." "Marriage lived *for* the glory of God." The topic is not: "The glory of God *for* the living of marriage." And not: "Marriage lived *by* the glory of God." But: "Marriage lived *for* the glory of God."

This little word means that there is an order of priority. There is an order of ultimacy. And the order is plain: God is ultimate and marriage is not. God is the most important Reality; marriage is less important—far less important, infinitely less important. Marriage exists to magnify the truth and worth and beauty and greatness of God; God does not exist to magnify marriage. Until this order is vivid and valued—until it is seen and savored—marriage will not be experienced as a revelation of God's glory but as a rival of God's glory.

I take my topic, "Marriage lived for the glory of God," to be an answer to the question: Why marriage? Why is there marriage? Why does marriage exist? Why do we live in marriages? This means that my topic is part of a larger question: Why does anything exist? Why do you exist? Why does sex exist? Why do earth and sun and moon and stars exist? Why do animals and plants and oceans and mountains and atoms and galaxies exist? The answer to all these questions, including the one about marriage is: All of them exist to and for the glory of God.

That is, they exist to magnify the truth and worth and beauty and greatness of God. Not the way a *microscope* magnifies, but the way a *telescope* magnifies. Microscopes magnify by making tiny things look bigger than they are. Telescopes magnify by making unimaginably big things look like what they really are. Microscopes move the appearance of size away from reality. Telescopes move the appearance of size toward reality. When I say that all things exist to magnify the truth and worth and beauty and greatness of God, I mean that all things—and marriage in particular—exist to move the appearance of God in people's minds toward Reality.

God is unimaginably great and infinitely valuable and unsurpassed in beauty. "Great is the LORD, and greatly to be praised, and his greatness is unsearchable" (Ps. 145:3, ESV). Everything that exists is meant to magnify that Reality. God cries out through the prophet Isaiah (43:6-7, ESV), "Bring my sons from afar and my daughters from the end of the earth, everyone who is called by my name, whom I cre- ated *for my glory*" (emphasis added). We have been created to display the glory of God. Paul concludes the first eleven chapters of his great letter to the Romans with the exaltation of God as the source and end of all things: "For from him and through him and *to him* are all things. To him be glory forever. Amen" (11:36, ESV, emphasis added). He makes it even clearer in Colossians 1:16, where he says, "By [Christ] all things were created, in heaven and on earth . . . all things were cre- ated through him and *for him*" (emphasis added).

And woe to us if we think that "for Him" means "for His need," or "for His benefit," or "for His improvement." Paul made it crystal clear in Acts 17:25 that God is not "served by human hands, as though he needed anything, since he himself gives to all mankind life and breath and everything" (ESV). No, the term "for His glory" and "for Him" means, "for the display of His glory," or "for the showing of His glory," or "for the magnifying of His glory."

We need to let this sink in. Once there was God, and only God.

The universe is His creation. It is not coeternal with God. It is not God. "In the beginning was the Word, and the Word was with God, and the Word was God. . . . All things were made through him" (John 1:1, 3, ESV). All things. All that is not God was made by God. So once there was only God.

Therefore God is absolute Reality. We are not. The universe is not. Marriage is not. We are derivative. The universe is of secondary importance, not primary. The human race is not the ultimate reality, nor the ultimate value, nor the ultimate measuring rod of what is good or what is true or what is beautiful. God is. God is the one ultimate absolute in existence. Everything else is from Him and through Him and for Him.

That is the starting place for understanding marriage. If we get this wrong, everything goes wrong. And if we get it right—really right, in our heads and in our hearts—then marriage will be transformed by it. Marriage will become what it was created by God to be—a display of the truth and worth and beauty and greatness of God.

This leads to a very simple conclusion—so simple and yet so far-reaching. If we want to see marriage have the place in the world and in the church that it is supposed to have—that is, if we want marriage to glorify the truth and worth and beauty and greatness of God—we must teach and preach less about marriage and more about God.

Most young people today do not bring to their courtship and marriage a great vision of God—who He is, what He is like, how He acts. In the world there is almost no vision of God. He is not even on the list to be invited. He is simply and breathtakingly omitted. And in the church the view of God that young couples bring to their relationship is so small instead of huge, and so marginal instead of central, and so vague instead of clear, and so impotent instead of all-determining, and so uninspiring instead of ravishing, that when they marry, the thought of living marriage to the glory of God is without meaning and without content.

What would the "glory of God" mean to a young wife or husband who gives almost no time and no thought to knowing the glory of God, or the glory of Jesus Christ, His divine Son . . .

• the glory of His *eternality* that makes the mind want to explode with the infinite thought that God never had a beginning, but simply always was;

• the glory of His *knowledge* that makes the Library of Congress look like a matchbox and quantum physics like a first grade reader;

• the glory of His *wisdom* that has never been and can never be counseled by men;

• the glory of His *authority* over heaven and earth and hell, without whose permission no man and no demon can move one inch;

• the glory of His *providence* without which not one bird falls to the ground or a single hair turns gray;

• the glory of His *word* that upholds the universe and keeps all the atoms and molecules together;

• the glory of His *power* to walk on water, cleanse lepers, heal the lame, open the eyes of the blind, cause the deaf to hear, still storms with a word, and raise the dead;

• the glory of His *purity* never to sin, or to have a two-second bad attitude or evil thought;

• the glory of His *trustworthiness* never to break His word or let one promise fall to the ground;

• the glory of His *justice* to render all moral accounts in the universe settled either on the cross or in hell;

• the glory of His *patience* to endure our dullness for decade after decade;

• the glory of His sovereign, slave-like *obedience* to embrace the excruciating pain of the cross willingly;

• the glory of His *wrath* that will one day cause people to call out for the rocks and the mountains to fall on them;

• the glory of His *grace* that justifies the ungodly; and

• the glory of His *love* that dies for us even while we were sinners.

How are people going to live their lives so that their marriages display the truth and worth and beauty and greatness of this glory, when they devote almost no energy or time to knowing and cherishing this glory?

Perhaps you can see why over the last twenty years of pastoral ministry I have come to see my life-mission and the mission of our church in some very basic terms: namely, I exist—we exist—to spread a passion for the supremacy of God in all things for the joy of all peoples. That's our assessment of the need. Until there is a passion for the supremacy and the glory of God in the hearts of married people, marriage will not be lived for the glory of God.

And there will not be a passion for the supremacy and the glory of God in the hearts of married people until God Himself, in His manifold glories, is known. And He will not be known in His manifold glories until pastors and teachers speak of Him tirelessly and constantly and deeply and biblically and faithfully and distinctly and thoroughly and passionately. Marriage lived for the glory of God will be the fruit of churches permeated with the glory of God.

So I say again, if we want marriage to glorify the truth and worth and beauty and greatness of God, we must teach and preach less about marriage and more about God. Not that we preach too much on marriage, but that we preach too little on God. God is simply not magnificently central in the lives of most of our people. He is not the sun around which all the planets of our daily lives are held in orbit and find their proper, God-appointed place. He is more like the moon, which waxes and wanes, and you can go for nights and never think about Him.

For most of our people, God is marginal and a hundred good things usurp His place. To think that their marriages could be lived for His glory by teaching on the dynamics of relationships, when the glory of God is so peripheral, is like expecting the human eye to glorify the stars when we don't stare at the night sky and have never bought a telescope.

So knowing God and cherishing God and valuing the glory of God above all things, including your spouse, is the key to living marriage to the glory of God. It's true in marriage, as in every other relationship: God is most glorified in us when we are most satisfied in Him.

Here is a key that unlocks a thousand doors. Superior satisfaction in God above all earthly things, including your spouse and your health and your own life (Psalm 63:3, ESV, "your steadfast love is better than life") is the source of great long-suffering without which husbands cannot love like Christ, and wives cannot follow like the bride of Christ, the church. Ephesians 5:22-25 makes plain that husbands take their cues of leadership and love from Christ, and wives take their cues of submission and love from the devotion of the church for whom He died. And both of those complementary acts of love—to lead, and to submit—are unsustainable for the glory of God without a superior satisfaction in all that God is for us in Christ.

Let me say it another way. There are two levels at which the glory of God may shine forth from a Christian marriage:

One is at the structural level when both spouses fulfill the roles God intended for them—the man as leader like Christ, the wife as advocate and follower of that leadership. When those roles are lived out, the glory of God's love and wisdom in Christ is displayed to the world.

But there is another deeper, more foundational level where the glory of God must shine if these roles are to be sustained as God designed. The power and impulse to carry through the self-denial and daily, monthly, yearly dying that will be required in loving an imperfect wife and loving an imperfect husband must come from a hope-giving, soul-sustaining, superior satisfaction in God. I don't think that our love for our wives or theirs for us will glorify God until it flows from a heart that delights in God more than marriage. Marriage will be preserved for the glory of God and shaped for the glory of God when the glory of God is more precious to us than marriage.

When we can say with the apostle Paul (in Philippians 3:8), "I count all things to be loss in view of the surpassing value of knowing Christ Jesus my Lord" (NASB)—when we can say that about marriage—about our husband or wife—then that marriage will be lived to the glory of God.

I close by trying to say this one more way, namely, with a poem that I wrote for my son on his wedding day.

LOVE HER MORE AND LOVE HER LESS

For Karsten Luke Piper
At His Wedding to
Rochelle Ann Orvis
May 29, 1995

The God whom we have loved, and in
Whom we have lived, and who has been
Our Rock these twenty-two good years
With you, now bids us, with sweet tears,
To let you go: "A man shall leave
His father and his mother, cleave
Henceforth unto his wife, and be
One unashaméd flesh and free."
This is the word of God today,
And we are happy to obey.
For God has given you a bride
Who answers every prayer we've cried
For over twenty years, our claim
For you, before we knew her name.

And now you ask that I should write
A poem—a risky thing, in light
Of what you know: that I am more
The preacher than the poet or
The artist. I am honored by
Your bravery, and I comply.
I do not grudge these sweet confines
Of rhyming pairs and metered lines.
They are old friends. They like it when
I bid them help me once again
To gather feelings into form
And keep them durable and warm.

And so we met in recent days,
And made the flood of love and praise
And counsel from a father's heart
To flow within the banks of art.

Here is a portion of the stream,
My son: a sermon poem. Its theme:
A double rule of love that shocks;
A doctrine in a paradox:

If you now aim your wife to bless,
Then love her more and love her less.

If in the coming years, by some
Strange providence of God, you come
To have the riches of this age,
And, painless, stride across the stage
Beside your wife, be sure in health
To love her, love her more than wealth.

And if your life is woven in
A hundred friendships, and you spin
A festal fabric out of all
Your sweet affections, great and small,
Be sure, no matter how it rends,
To love her, love her more than friends.

And if there comes a point when you
Are tired, and pity whispers, "Do
Yourself a favor. Come, be free;
Embrace the comforts here with me."
Know this! Your wife surpasses these:
So love her, love her more than ease.

And when your marriage bed is pure,
And there is not the slightest lure
Of lust for any but your wife,
And all is ecstasy in life,
A secret all of this protects:
Go love her, love her more than sex.

And if your taste becomes refined,
And you are moved by what the mind
Of man can make, and dazzled by

His craft, remember that the "why"
Of all this work is in the heart;
So love her, love her more than art.

And if your own should someday be
The craft that critics all agree
Is worthy of a great esteem,
And sales exceed your wildest dream,
Beware the dangers of a name.
And love her, love her more than fame.

And if, to your surprise, not mine,
God calls you by some strange design
To risk your life for some great cause,
Let neither fear nor love give pause,
And when you face the gate of death,
Then love her, love her more than breath.

Yes, love her, love her, more than life;
Oh, love the woman called your wife.
Go love her as your earthly best.
Beyond this venture not. But, lest
Your love become a fool's facade,
Be sure to love her less than God.

It is not wise or kind to call
An idol by sweet names, and fall,
As in humility, before
A likeness of your God. Adore
Above your best beloved on earth
The God alone who gives her worth.
And she will know in second place
That your great love is also grace,
And that your high affections now
Are flowing freely from a vow
Beneath these promises, first made
To you by God. Nor will they fade
For being rooted by the stream

Of Heaven's Joy, which you esteem
And cherish more than breath and life,
That you may give it to your wife.

The greatest gift you give your wife
Is loving God above her life.
And thus I bid you now to bless:
Go love her more by loving less.

4

The Husband as Prophet, Priest, and King[1]

Bob Lepine

———∞∞∞———

Just what does the Bible mean when it teaches in 1 Corinthians 11 that the man is the head of the woman? Sadly, throughout the history of the church, the concept of a man as head of his wife has been misunderstood, misinterpreted, and misapplied by pastors and Bible teachers. As a consequence, many husbands have used this biblical idea as license for harsh treatment, a lack of love and compassion, and even abuse of their wives. They seem to have learned more about headship from the Pharaohs of Egypt than from the Lamb of God.

Women have rightly rebelled against dictatorship in marriage. It is clear to them that whatever headship means, it doesn't mean a harsh or unloving attitude but a spirit of kindness and compassion. It doesn't mean selfishness, but self-sacrifice. It doesn't mean control, but a willingness to assume responsibility.

The way in which the biblical concept of headship has been abused in the church does not mean, however, that the Bible can be ignored here. Certainly, biblical passages have been misunderstood and misapplied in a way that has devalued a woman's role in the home and in the church. But those abuses are not grounds for ignoring or reinventing meanings for difficult biblical passages. Our goal should be to better understand the way in which Christ serves as head of His church, or in which God is the head of Christ, in order to know how a husband should be the head of his wife.

In his *Institutes,* John Calvin said that "the office which [Christ] received from the Father consists of three parts. For he was appointed . . . Prophet, King and Priest."[2] Christ's headship, according to Calvin, involves the perfect fulfillment of the Old Testament types. He is, according to the author of Hebrews, our high priest and eternal king, after the order of Melchizedek (Heb. 6:20; 7:1-2), and God's prophet during the last days (Heb. 1:1-2). Further, the messianic title of Christ ("anointed one") refers to the anointing with holy oil that was, under the Law, given to prophets, priests, and kings.

Today, Christ is the head of His church by serving as prophet, priest, and king. If a husband is to be the head of his wife in the same way that Christ is the head of the church, then as a husband he must understand the prophetic, priestly, and kingly roles he is to fulfill.

THE HUSBAND AS A PRIEST

A husband is, by God's design, the priest of his family. This was clear to the patriarchs of Israel, who assumed a priestly role by interceding for their families, as Abraham did when God announced His judgment of Sodom, and by offering sacrifices to Yahweh. Noah, after seeing the wrath of God poured out, called his sons together as soon as they were on dry land to offer a sacrifice to God. The patriarchs, who were the family and tribal leaders in ancient Israel, knew they had a duty to lead their wives and children into God's presence for worship, to remind them of God's grace and mercy in forgiving their sins, and to intercede on their behalf. Husbands today have the same priestly assignment.

When our children were a year or two old, Mary Ann and I sometimes found ourselves on long trips with a crying child in the car seat. During one such trip, I was trying to find some way to quiet our daughter, and I launched into an a cappella version of "It Is Well with My Soul." The sound of singing startled Amy enough to stop her crying momentarily. Mary Ann joined in on the second line. Before long, the novelty of our singing wore off, and Amy was back to full volume.

As she got louder, so did we. It took ten or fifteen minutes of "Crown Him with Many Crowns" and "All Hail the Power of Jesus' Name," but Amy finally fell asleep. But we were having a great time singing psalms, hymns, and spiritual songs, making melody in our hearts and on our lips (Eph. 5:19).

In the same way that the priests in the Old Testament superintended the worship of the Israelites, a husband should function as the worship leader for his marriage. That involves more than singing hymns or praise choruses in the car, of course! A husband should be the one to initiate prayer with his wife, not only at meals but throughout the day. He should be the one to make regular church attendance a family priority. He should be the one to read the Scriptures to his wife and children. These are the kinds of regular habits that a husband ought to initiate, beginning on the first morning of the honeymoon!

Too many husbands assume that their spiritual leadership in this area will begin once the children are older. In truth it begins the day the spiritual responsibility for a young woman is passed from her father to her husband. In our contemporary, individualistic, egalitarian culture, many husbands reject their priestly responsibilities with their wives (I was one of them), thinking, *She's fully capable of having her own quiet time or doing her own Bible reading. Besides, I'll just embarrass myself.* The mature, godly man will not shy away. He will assume that his role as priest for his wife is a necessary function of being called her husband.

A husband-priest is also responsible before God to be an intercessor. He has the responsibility and privilege to speak to God on behalf of his wife. It is not that she doesn't have access to the throne of grace herself. She has the same privileges in the heavenly courts as her husband. The Bible teaches that all believers are part of a "royal priesthood" (1 Pet. 2:9), and that there is no intermediary between man and God except for the man Christ Jesus (1 Tim. 2:5). Still, if a man aspires to be a godly husband, he will assume responsibility to oversee the spiritual condition of his wife. To love and serve his wife as Christ loves His church, a husband must intercede on her behalf. In John 17, where Jesus intercedes for His followers, we find a pattern of intercession a husband can follow in praying for his wife:

1. Begin by praying that God would be glorified in and through her life. Above all else, a husband should pray for what brings glory to God.

2. Next, a husband ought to pray that his wife will know God. The apostle Paul prayed for himself, "that I may know Him and the power of His resurrection and the fellowship of His sufferings, being conformed to His death; in order that I may attain to the resurrection from the dead" (Phil. 3:10-11, NASB). A husband can ask the Lord that his wife might grow in her knowledge of God and her depth of insight (Phil. 1:9).

3. A husband ought to pray for God's protection, physically and spiritually, for his wife. He can pray that God would protect her as she walks to her car in the parking lot at the mall, or as she drives the kids to soccer practice in rush hour traffic. But more than that, a husband ought to pray that his wife will hold fast to her faith, even in the midst of difficult times or persecution.

4. A husband ought to pray for his wife to grow in holiness, sanctified by the truth of God's Word (John 17:17). His desire should be that his wife would be set apart and useful in God's service. This may be hard for a husband to pray, because his wife's life might reflect a higher commitment to holiness than his own! If so, it should challenge him to a new level of personal holiness.

5. A husband ought to ask God that he and his wife would be of one heart and one mind in their relationship with each other. He can pray that they would continue to draw closer to each other, rather than yielding to the temptations to drift apart that all couples experience. When he is experiencing conflict with his wife, he can pray for God to intervene. John Yates, in his helpful book *How a Man Prays for His Family*, encourages every husband to pray diligently that God would move him and his wife toward unity in their marriage. "If your wife has irritating habits or attitudes," Yates writes, "it is possible that you—her husband, lover, supporter—are not the right person to bring about those changes in her life. But you can, as a prayer partner, work on these things by talking to God about them and seeking His help on her behalf."[3]

6. He can also pray that his wife would find companions and soul-mates who share not only her faith in Christ but also her convictions about how to live as a godly woman and godly wife. He can pray that the Enemy would not disrupt those relationships. A wife needs the strength that comes from solid relationships with others in the body of Christ, who share what the apostle Peter called "a faith of the same kind as ours" (2 Pet. 1:1).

THE HUSBAND AS A PROPHET

As part of the headship responsibility, every husband also bears the call to be a prophet in the home. In its simplest definition, a "prophet" is "one who speaks for God." Although this may conjure up images of fortune-tellers, miracle workers, or locust-eating preachers, the prophet of God has always been one who speaks the word of the Lord.

Author and counselor Dan Allender offers a helpful definition of what it means to serve Christ as a prophet today. "He is a bearer of the word of God," Allender writes, "a spokesman for righteousness, a poet of hope. . . . The true prophet disturbs and invites the heart to return to godly worship. In fact, the prophet is a servant of the church who stands outside the church in order to invite those who appear to be in it to return to true worship."[4]

Here are some marks of a prophetic husband:

He hears from God. The prophet, as Allender said, is one who bears the word of God. Before he can speak on God's behalf, he must be a man who hears clearly the word of God, so that he might faithfully pass it on to his wife and children.

The author of Hebrews reminds us that God "spoke long ago to the fathers in the prophets in many portions and in many ways" (Heb. 1:1, NASB). These prophets heard directly from God in dreams, visions, through an audible voice, or through an impression in their spirit. Today, we have the completed revelation of God in the pages of the Bible. To hear from God today, a husband must diligently equip himself as a student of the Scriptures. Douglas Wilson, in his book *Reforming Marriage,* says:

a man may not be a vocational theologian, but in his home he must be the resident theologian. The apostle Paul, when he is urging women to keep silent in the church, tells them that "if they want to learn something, let them ask their own husbands at home" (1 Corinthians 14:35). The tragedy is that many modern women have to wonder why the Bible says they should have to ask their husbands. . . . a husband must be prepared to answer his wife's doctrinal questions, and if he cannot, then he must be prepared to study so that he can remedy the deficiency.[5]

We think of a prophet as one who proclaims Gods truth. He is first and foremost one who hears from God so that he can proclaim the truth accurately. A husband who would attempt to speak on God's behalf should tremble at the assignment. After all, false prophets in the Old Testament were stoned. The New Testament warns us to "be diligent to present yourself approved to God as a workman who does not need to be ashamed, handling accurately the word of truth" (2 Tim. 2:15, NASB).

He establishes a doctrinal foundation for his home. We live in an age when doctrine is viewed negatively. You may have heard preachers say, "You don't need doctrine, you just need Jesus!" Doctrine is viewed as rigid, stuffy, boring, divisive, and almost antithetical to the cause of Christ.

In truth, there is no understanding of the Scriptures or of who Jesus is without some understanding of theology and doctrine. When talking with a friend who was "down" on doctrine, I asked simply, "Who is this Jesus in whom you claim to believe?" Puzzled by such an obvious question, he said, "He's the Son of God, the Savior of the world!" "No, no, no," I protested. "I don't want theology! Don't give me that doctrinal stuff! Just tell me who Jesus is!"

The point quickly became obvious to my friend. Whenever we express basic truths of the Christian faith, we are dealing with doctrine. Theology is a word that literally means "the study of God." Rather than ignoring theological and doctrinal issues, dismissing them as foolish or unnecessary, a husband should find himself wrestling with the issues raised in Scripture and should determine for his wife and his family what is right and true.

Wilson astutely observes that husbands are to blame for the theological breakdown in the church today. "The evangelical world," he writes, "is throwing away its theological heritage because of doctrinal faithlessness in Christian homes. It is true that pulpits across our country are filled with a swamp and morass of anecdotes, sentimentalist yawp, yippy-skippy worship, and make-it-up-as-you-go-along theology; but the heads of Christian homes have been willing to have it so. As the expectations for men in the evangelical world have gotten lower, men have not objected—they have breathed a sigh of relief."[6]

In his *Institutes,* John Calvin referred to a prophet as a supplier of useful doctrine. In addition to hearing from God, a husband should fill that role in his home.

He faithfully proclaims the truth of God. On long drives, late at night, when the kids are sleeping in the back, Mary Ann and I have found ourselves reviewing things we've learned together in church, or rehearsing concepts we've picked up from reading or from listening to tapes. "What is the Latin phrase that means 'at once sinful and justified?'" I'll ask.

"I'm too tired to play this," she'll say.

"I'm too tired not to play!" I'll coax her. "Help me stay awake."

We'll mentally review books of the Bible, or we'll toss out a verse and see if the other one knows where it is found. We may listen to a teaching tape and discuss what we've heard. As the drive wears on, the game will usually deteriorate to the point where I'm asking questions like, "Name three hits by Herman's Hermits."

For many Christian men, the idea of some formal time of Bible study or instruction with our wives is in our "top ten" list of threatening activities. We feel inadequate and unsure of ourselves. We're not sure how to do it or what to say when we're finished. We're not eloquent like the pastor. We're afraid we'll be exposed for what we don't know, or for the shallowness of our own spirituality, or that we'll be convicted of hypocrisy by a wife who knows too well that we don't always practice what we're preaching. So many of us have abandoned any attempt to lead our wives in any kind of informal study of the Scriptures. We may make a stab at some kind of family devotions once the children are old enough to sit still, but as they squirm or stare out the window, most fathers throw in the towel and give up the whole idea.

A husband needs to muster his courage and take the initiative regularly to call his wife and family back to the Scriptures as their source of life and truth. He doesn't have to rely on his own insights or creativity. There are tools, like Dennis and Barbara Rainey's devotional *Moments Together for Couples,* or the daily devotional magazine *Tabletalk,* produced by Ligonier Ministries, which a husband and wife can read together. A husband can stand on the shoulders of others as he fulfills his prophetic responsibility to declare the truth of the Scriptures to his wife.

He confronts sin and calls his wife to repentance. Perhaps this is the most difficult assignment facing a husband, for several reasons. First, confronting sin and calling a wife to repentance may rock the domestic boat. A husband may decide he doesn't want to incur his wife's wrath. But he needs to obey God's call regardless of how his wife will respond.

He may also fail to confront his wife's sin because he has a soft view of what it means to love her. Pointing out sin seems harsh and judgmental, not loving. But our example here is Christ, who loves us too much to overlook our sin. The same Prophet who wept over Jerusalem, pronouncing judgment on Israel, comes to us today by His Holy Spirit to convict us of our sin and to lead us to righteousness. If we begin to understand the consequences of sin for ourselves and for future generations, we will not think it loving to ignore or overlook our wives' ongoing patterns of sinful behavior.

A husband-prophet may also feel hypocritical pointing out the speck in his wife's eye when he is aware of his own sinfulness. But Jesus' instructions were clear on this. It is not necessarily hypocrisy to confront someone else about her sin; it becomes hypocrisy when you do so without first confessing and repenting of your own sin. "First," Jesus said, "take the log out of your own eye, and then you will see clearly to take the speck out of your brother's eye" (Matt. 7:5).

It is easy to see why husbands would rather not confront the sinful behavior of their wives. (I include myself in their number!) Most books I've read on how to have a happy marriage don't suggest that one of the keys is confronting sin in your mate. But we are reminded in Proverbs that the wounds of a friend are faithful (Prov. 27:6). If our goal is the glory of God, happiness in marriage will at times need to take a back seat to the higher calling of helping our wives—our sisters in Christ—to be conformed to Christ's likeness.

THE HUSBAND AS A KING

We have seen how a husband is called by God to be both prophet and priest to his wife. Now we come to the discussion of the husband as king. Because of the many ways this subject has been abused by well-meaning but ill-informed Bible teachers, we need to proceed with caution.

Those of us who live in a democracy may think of a king as someone who wields power and who enjoys privilege and position. For example, we Americans can see the British royal family as having no real responsibilities other than the ceremonial, and leading a life where any material need is fulfilled on command. From American shores, it appears as the ultimate in selfish indulgence.

In ancient Israel, however, though the kings were wealthy their function was much more than ceremonial. In their quarrel with the prophet Samuel over their desire to be ruled by a king, Israel said, "there shall be a king over us, that we also may be like all the nations, *that our king may judge us and go out before us and fight our battles*" (1 Sam. 8:19-20, NASB, emphasis added). Author Dan Allender expands that idea:

> The king led, protected and provided for the safety of the realm. He secured the infrastructure necessary for civilization. He justly applied the law of God to the government, commerce and care of the state. . . . The king was not only a warrior, but he also was the representative of the realm in conversations with the "world." He planned strategies, negotiated alliances, and applied the word of God to daily conflicts. . . . In so doing, he became the one who took the truth of God into the world and invited unbelievers to know and bow before the God of Israel.[7]

Those are the same responsibilities God has assigned to a husband. He is to lead his wife. He is her provider. He is her protector.

He is to know and apply the law of God in the home. A husband is responsible to represent his wife and his family in the culture.

In His incarnation, Jesus was revealed not only as the perfect prophet of God and our great high priest but also as king of heaven and earth. He is once again our model for how we as husbands are to rule in our homes. For the sake of our wives, we must assume our true kingly role and lead with humble hearts and loving service for our wives. Here are some practical steps a husband can take as he seeks to take on the mantle of a servant-king:

Examine your leadership. As a husband, have you abused the leadership and authority God has entrusted to you? Do you have a tendency to be a self-serving, domineering leader? Do you recognize that as a distortion of God's design?

Or have you instead been passive? Have you disengaged from the responsibility to lead your home and your family, leaving your wife to assume that position?

Or have you taken on the responsibility of serving your wife without accepting the responsibility to lead her?

You're in there somewhere. Almost certainly, you have a natural, sinful pattern that characterizes your leadership. When you slip up as a husband, you probably find yourself slipping in the same direction over and over again. God wants to steady your footing. It begins by agreeing with Him that you have a tendency to be either a domineering or a passive leader—or a husband who only serves without also leading.

God is calling us as husbands to repent, to change! We are to lock our sites on the example of the perfect Leader, and then follow in His footsteps. As we grow in our understanding of our role as king, and as we begin to apply the truth of Scripture in our marriage, God will make us into the kind of leaders He has called us to become.

Start leading! I've never forgotten a quote I read once, attributed to C. S. Lewis (although I've never been able to pinpoint the source). "The best way to acquire a virtue," he is reported to have said, "is to act as if you already have it."

As husband and wife, it's time to sit down and begin to discuss areas in your marriage where you need to start showing some leadership. Ask your wife to point out areas where you can be leading her and your family. Examine the major areas—your faith, your marriage, your family, your job, your relationships with friends, your service to the community, your physical health and well-being, your stewardship over the resources God has given you, and your recreational time—and decide where you need to begin to take some initiative and lead.

As you lead, make sure to check your heart. Are you making decisions that will bring honor and glory to Christ and that will lead you and your wife to grow in your relationship with Him? Do you stand to gain personally from the decisions you're making? Remember, when you exercise your leadership for selfish purposes, you're abusing the important responsibility God has given you.

Do some strategic planning. Most successful businesses have a strategic plan, mapping out where the company is headed over the next five to ten years. Things change, of course, and the businesses adapt. They work hard to consider market conditions, examine competing organizations, access their own strengths and weaknesses, look for opportunities on the horizon, and then set the course for their businesses.

Many of those same businessmen, who can establish a successful plan for a company, are clueless when it comes to thinking strategically about the spiritual, emotional, physical, and social needs of their wives. Ask them about their five-year plan for their marriage and you're likely to get a deer-in-the-headlights look.

In their book *Intimate Allies,* Dan Allender and Tremper Longman III write about this aspect of how a husband should function as king in marriage: "We are called to cultivate Christ in our spouses. . . . To do so effectively, we must be guided by a vision of who they are, a picture of who they were meant to be [like Christ] and a grasp of our role in helping them become like Christ."[8]

During a "FamilyLife Today" radio interview about the book, Allender talked about writing a short-term mission statement for his wife. When he began explaining the idea, I thought it sounded presumptuous. But as Dan talked about encouraging and exhorting his wife to become all God wants her to be as a woman, as a wife, and as a mother, it was clear he was not being presumptuous. He was being the kind of kingly husband his wife ultimately wants and needs him to be.

Gentlemen, it's up to us. Have we prayerfully sought to map out a plan for the next five years of our marriage? It's time to look ahead and make some plans.

Know your enemy. The attacks on your marriage and on your leadership will come from all directions. They will come from a culture that is increasingly drifting away from God's standards and may be pulling your marriage along in its undertow. They will come from friends and coworkers who, thinking themselves to be wise, have become as fools (Rom. 1:22).

The attacks will come from some surprising places. Today, there are many evangelical churches that have lost their confessional moorings and their confidence in the absolute standards of God's Word. It shouldn't surprise you to hear popular "Christian" ideas about a husband's role in marriage—coming from books, radio, television, and even from church pulpits—that are not rooted in biblical truth. A wise husband will test everything he reads or hears—even this book—against the absolute standard of the Bible.

There will also be attacks from your closest ally, your wife. While her spirit will welcome the leadership, protection, and provision of a wise king, her flesh will war against her spirit and will seek to thwart your authority. Over time, there will be showdowns as you wrestle with whether to compromise and gain her approval or to stand fast and face her wrath. There will be times when you'll have to decide whether to serve her or to serve God.

Perhaps the greatest source of attack, as you seek to be faithful to God's calling as a husband, will come from your own flesh. You will slip into patterns and habits that come from years of living in rebellion against the things of God. You'll lack the confidence to lead. You'll lack the desire to serve. You'll look around and think, *I'm doing better than most husbands,* and you'll settle for less than God's best.

The apostle Paul knew that the issue of authority and submission was a spiritual minefield. In that specific context he warns all

Christians to "be strong in the Lord, and in the strength of His might. Put on the full armor of God, that you may be able to stand firm against the schemes of the devil" (Eph. 6:10-11, NASB). God has made provision for you to be able to stand strong in the face of opposition to His plan.

How are you doing as a husband who loves and leads your wife as Christ loves and leads His church? Using this report card, give yourself a letter grade in the following areas:

HUSBAND
REPORT CARD

Be on the alert, stand firm in the faith, act like men, be strong. Let all that you do be done in love (1 Cor. 16:13).

Priest:
- Leading in worship _____
- Intercession _____
- Reminding my wife of God's grace and mercy _____

Prophet
- Hearing from God _____
- Setting a doctrinal foundation for the home _____
- Proclaiming God's truth _____
- Confronting sin _____
- Reminding my wife of God's love for her _____

King
- Visionary leadership _____
- Sacrificial service _____
- Providing for needs
  Spiritual _____
  Physical _____
  Emotional _____
- Protecting my wife
  Spiritually _____
  Physically _____
  Emotionally _____

NOTES

1. The ideas on which this chapter is based were originally developed for Bob Lepine, *The Christian Husband* (Ann Arbor, Mich.: Servant, 1999).

2. John Calvin, *The Institutes of the Christian Religion,* trans. Henry Beveridge (Grand Rapids, Mich.: Eerdmans, 1993), book 2, chap. XV:1 (425-426).

3. John Yates, *How a Man Prays for His Family* (Minneapolis: Bethany, 1996), 92.

4. Dan Allender, "Mimicking Our Disruptive Father and Our Diverse Older Brother," *Mars Hill Review* 5 (Summer 1996), 41.

5. Douglas Wilson, *Reforming Marriage* (Moscow, Idaho: Canon, 1995), 33-34.

6. *Ibid.,* 32

7. Allender, "Mimicking Our Disruptive Father," 44.

8. Dan Allender and Tremper Longman III, *Intimate Allies* (Wheaton, Ill.: Tyndale, 1995), 89.

5

A Song of Joy:
Sexual Intimacy
in Marriage

C. J. Mahaney

———⊰⊱———

It was his magnum opus, the best and most important work he had ever conceived. In his lifetime, this prolific and gifted composer would write more than a thousand songs and hymns. Raised a prince, the son of a legendary king, and now a great king himself, he would be esteemed—by no less an authority than the very Word of God—as the wisest man who had ever lived. Now, this man of unsurpassed wisdom and exceptional creativity had completed his greatest song, a song above every song he had ever written or ever would write. King Solomon finished the final manuscript, set down his pen, and reviewed with satisfaction the fitting title: "Song of Songs."

It was about sex.

It was, more specifically, an explicit and unblushing celebration of sexual relations under the covenant of marriage, of unbridled, uninhibited, joyous immersion in passionate acts of physical love between a husband and wife. And one day, the lyrics to this song would be counted among the perfect and infallible words of Scripture, inerrantly inspired by the Holy Spirit and intended by God as a primary source of guidance for mankind until the return of the Son.

INTERPRETING THE SONG

Sincere Christians, many of them far more mature and knowledgeable than I, may hold a different interpretation of this book. They may understand it to be primarily, if not exclusively, an allegory or typology of the relationship between Christ and the church, or of Christ and the soul of the individual believer. Before proceeding, it seems appropriate for me to clarify my perspective and its rationale.

As may already be apparent, I take the Song of Songs at face value. A plain reading of the book indicates to me that it is about two human beings: a man and a woman. I believe that, in the inspiration of this book, the Holy Spirit had in view the relationship between a husband and wife. This book celebrates and teaches about romance and the gift of sex. At no point does Scripture suggest to me that an alternative interpretation of Solomon's Song is necessary or preferable. I do insist, of course, on limiting the application of this celebration of human sexuality to heterosexual marriage, but that is simply to observe the full and clear counsel of Scripture on the subject.

Perhaps the allegorical view is adopted by some because of the explicit content of Solomon's Song. Such a reaction may be rooted in the belief that sex, even in the context of marriage, has been influenced by the Fall and is thus to be merely tolerated rather than celebrated. I don't see that position in the Bible. Indeed, several passages elsewhere in Scripture plainly celebrate marital relations as a source of legitimate godly joy and satisfaction.

Moreover, the Song of Songs is suffused with erotic content between this man and woman, but there is no suggestion in Scripture that the relationship between God and humans is ever to be understood as having an erotic component. ("God is Spirit, and his worshipers must worship in spirit and in truth" [John 4:24, NIV].) Although the marriage between Christ and His Bride will be many unimaginably wonderful things, it will not be sexual as we understand the term. Extraordinarily and supernaturally intimate. Infinitely rewarding and fulfilling. But not physically erotic. Physical eroticism, while a wonderful gift from God when rightly enjoyed, is a gift of limited duration. It is a gift to married couples, to be enjoyed for as long as they both shall live.

I don't believe the Song of Solomon is allegory or typology. I don't believe it is drama. I do not believe it is history, or a description of Solomon's experience. I agree with Tom Gledhill's perspective: "The two lovers are Everyman and Everywoman and have nothing to do with Solomon."[1]

The Song of Songs is unique: an entire book of the Bible devoted to the celebration of romance and sexual love within marriage. Lloyd Carr has written, "It comes to us in this world of sin, where lust and passion are on every hand, where fierce temptations assail us and try to turn us aside from the God-given standard of marriage. And it reminds us, in particularly beautiful fashion, how pure and noble true love is."[2] Elsewhere he notes, "The lover and the beloved are just ordinary people."[3] That's encouraging. The Song is about us, about every husband and wife. It can speak to us, and in doing so make a dramatic difference in our lives. Let's look now, honestly and joyfully, at how God chose to elaborate in His holy Word on the gift of sexual relations.

BEYOND SWEET NOTHINGS: A DUET IN THE KEY OF ROMANCE

Even a casual reader of the Song of Songs is struck by the words and deeds of pure and passionate romance that adorn nearly every verse. I believe genuine romance, such as we find modeled here, is meant to be a growing reality within marriage, not a dimming memory. Husbands, it is our privilege, joy, and God-given responsibility to romance our wives—really romance our wives. As we look to this Song for guidance, we see that romance involves, at a minimum, communication and creativity.

Husbands: Verse One. This book is filled with verbal expressions of love between the lovers. The communication described in the Song of Songs is, quite simply, erotic from start to finish. This is neither idle chit-chat nor talking about daily practicalities like kids, carpools, and church. This is highly intentional, provocative language, whose purpose is to arouse romantic passion, to inflame, slowly and purposefully, all the while honoring and blessing one's spouse. It's hot stuff!

This approach, which would be divinely forbidden, scandalous, and deeply shameful in any other context, is encouraged and esteemed within marriage by Holy Scripture.

Duane Garrett writes of the lovers in the Song:

> They relish their pleasure in each other not only with physical action, but with carefully composed words. Love is, above all, a matter of the mind and heart and should be declared. The lesson for the reader is that he or she needs to speak often and openly of his or her joy in the beloved, the spouse. This is, for many lovers, a far more embarrassing revelation of the self than anything that is done with the body. But it is precisely here that the biblical ideal of love is present—in the uniting of the bodies and hearts of the husband and wife in a bond that is as strong as death. Many homes would be happier if men and women would simply speak of their love for one another a little more often.[4]

Indeed, articulate and carefully composed words of passion are modeled throughout the Song of Songs. Much of it, of course, is couched in the language of Near Eastern poetry, the idioms of which can seem foreign to us, even grotesque. But behind those decidedly non-Western turns of phrase there is wisdom and beauty.

"Your neck is like an ivory tower. Your eyes are the pools of Heshbon by the gate of Bath Rabbim. Your nose is like the tower of Lebanon looking toward Damascus" (7:4, NIV). Now, gentlemen, by all means do try this sort of thing at home—just don't use these exact phrases. Your wife is not likely to interpret direct quotes of this passage as complimentary, much less arousing of the kind of passions you had in mind. But what's being expressed here is, in fact, very positive. He is telling her that her nose is lovely and perfectly suited to her, that it ideally complements the rest of her face. In the cultural context in which Solomon wrote, these architectural allusions were, without question, tender and heartfelt expressions of deep admiration for her physical beauty. And that is how they would have been received.

But note this well. Throughout the passages in which one lover describes the body of the other—for, as we shall see, the woman also compliments her man in no uncertain terms—there is both beauty and brilliance. In these phrases, the most private emotions are expressed regarding the most intimate parts of a spouse's body. Above all, they are expressed appropriately, romantically, tastefully, and descriptively. There is in the Song of Songs the complete absence of any medical language, crudeness, or profanity. Every word is tender and sensual, and carefully composed to produce appropriate and passionate arousal.

The man speaks to his beloved: "I liken you, my darling, to a mare harnessed to one of the chariots of Pharaoh. Your cheeks are beautiful with earrings, your neck with strings of jewels. We will make you earrings of gold, studded with silver" (1:9-11, NIV). Notice how he begins: "My darling." He then moves on to an analogy that Westerners can thoroughly misconstrue. In commenting on the word "mare," one writer suggests that the woman must have had very large hips, suitable for childbearing. Another indicates she is no doubt a fast runner! But more accomplished scholarship reveals the beauty and the vibrant sexual overtones of this high compliment. It seems that mares were never employed to draw the king's chariot. Only stallions were, and they were always hitched in pairs. But in this picture, a mare has been harnessed to the chariot alongside a stallion. The predictable result is a stallion in a frenzy of galloping desire. When this man, then, speaks of his beloved using this analogy, it is not to suggest that she possesses equine characteristics but to declare the overwhelming sensual impact she makes upon him by her very presence. He then speaks of how her jewelry enhances the beauty of her face; together they will further complement her natural attractions with additional jewelry. (Christians will want to balance such passages with the teachings of 1 Peter 3, but clearly there is a place for the appropriate enhancement of physical beauty.)

Do you see the qualitative difference between such carefully composed words of romance and something like, "That dress looks nice on you, dear"? By all means, tell her that she looks nice in the dress, but recognize the world of difference between a simple compliment (however sincere) and phrases describing a passion that can barely be contained.

Let's look at one more passage of carefully composed words spoken by the man:

How beautiful you are, my darling! Oh, how beautiful! Your eyes behind your veil are doves. Your hair is like a flock of goats descending from Mount Gilead. Your teeth are like a flock of sheep just shorn, coming up from the washing. Each has its twin; not one of them is alone. Your lips are like a scarlet ribbon; your mouth is lovely. Your temples behind your veil are like the halves of a pomegranate. Your neck is like the tower of David, built with elegance; on it hang a thousand shields, all of them shields of warriors. Your two breasts are like two fawns, like twin fawns of a gazelle that browse among the lilies. Until the day breaks and the shadows flee, I will go to the mountain of myrrh and to the hill of incense. All beautiful you are, my darling; there is no flaw in you

—4:1-7, NIV

This magnificent passage begins with a declaration of the beauty of his beloved. But generalities are not enough for him, nor should they be for us. So, he extols her eyes, her hair, and her teeth, using clear and complimentary analogies. What creativity his words reveal! "Your eyes behind your veil are doves" speaks of her gentleness and tenderness. In describing her hair as a flock of goats descending from Mount Gilead, he evokes the image of a distant hill, completely covered with black-wooled goats moving toward its base, so the entire hill seems alive. Her teeth are white and fresh, like newly shorn and bathed sheep that glisten in the sun.

He then praises in specific, compelling, and poetic terms, her lips, mouth, and temples. He compares her lips to a precious, beautiful fabric. The Aramaic word he uses for her mouth makes clear that he finds her very speech a thing of beauty; her mouth reveals her heart, and her mouth is beautiful in no small part because of what she communicates. These compliments are not merely physical. They are mental and moral as well.

Gazing lower, he speaks in tender and radiant language of her neck and breasts, and with breathtaking delicacy and understatement he declares his unmistakably erotic intentions. He ends this love poem where he began, assuring her that, in his eyes, she is "all beautiful"—perfection itself.

"All beautiful," "no flaw in you"—how are we to interpret such phrases? No one need class these among those statements in the Old Testament which the apostle Paul found "hard to understand"! What's going on here is very clear. The man is lavishing high praises upon his beloved in an effort to communicate how he feels about her. These are expressions of his heartfelt emotion. Others may not share his assessment of her beauty. No matter. This is his view of her, and together they rejoice in it.

Wives: Verse Two. Wives, you too can find a wealth of example in Solomon's Song:

> *My lover is radiant and ruddy, outstanding among ten thousand. His head is purest gold; his hair is wavy and black as a raven. His eyes are like doves by the water streams, washed in milk, mounted like jewels. His cheeks are like beds of spice yielding perfume. His lips are like lilies dripping with myrrh. His arms are rods of gold. . . . His body is like polished ivory. . . . His legs are pillars of marble. . . . His appearance is like Lebanon. . . . His mouth is sweetness itself; he is altogether lovely. This is my lover, this is my friend, O daughters of Jerusalem.*
>
> —5:10-16, NIV

Here is an evaluation that few men could ever hope genuinely to warrant. So what is God saying in such passages? Is He setting impossibly narrow standards, such as the advertising and fashion industries would impose on us? Certainly not. Again, what's being communicated here is primarily the effect of the beloved on the lover. An objective description is clearly not the point at all! These are carefully composed words that convey her estimation of his value.

He is radiant: There is a joy and an inner contentment that shines through his face. He is ruddy: manly and masculine. He is outstanding: Place him in the midst of ten thousand others, and she can pick him out, for in her eyes he has no rival. His entire appearance is solid and firm, impressive like a mountain range. His mouth—that is, his speech—is lovely, and it also seems that she greatly enjoys his kisses.

Finally, she ends her praise with, "He is altogether lovely. This is my lover, this is my friend, O daughters of Jerusalem." With this triumphant declaration she invites the daughters of Jerusalem and all who read her words to agree with her. She is unconcerned that any might dare to dissent, for who would argue? This is how she feels! Nay-sayers may criticize her objectivity or precision, but even as they do they will envy the depth of love she enjoys and will find themselves, by contrast, far poorer than this blessed woman and her lover.

How my wife describes me bears little or no resemblance to how my male friends describe me. (Just one example: After teaching on this material in the church recently, a fellow pastor walked up to me after the message, glanced at my bald pate, and said, "Your head reminds me of the Jefferson Memorial.") And of course, it would be highly inappropriate for anyone but me to describe my wife using the kind of terms I would employ when declaring my love for her and reminding her of the effect she has on me.

The Song of Songs is a book about romance, and romance begins with carefully composed words of an emotional and erotic nature. How often in the past month has communication such as we find in Solomon's Song taken place between you and your spouse? What are the hindrances? What are the heart issues? What changes can you make this week to begin cultivating and expressing your passion for your spouse?

CREATIVE HARMONY: THE CONTEXT FOR ROMANCE

Last year, Carolyn and I celebrated our twenty-fifth wedding anniversary, and for that quarter-century it has been rare for us not to have a weekly date night. But I can assure you that the consistent cultivation of romance in our marriage has been far from an effortless process.

Romance must be diligently cultivated, lest it become routine. The wonderful security that comes from a context of covenant commitment is no excuse for the absence of romance. We should consistently express our passion for our spouse in a variety of creative ways. Date nights and other creative forms of romancing don't happen by themselves. They require regular, diligent, creative attention.

Where to begin? Husbands, study your wives. (Although husbands and wives need to understand this material equally well, this section will be directed primarily to the husband in his role as head of the wife.) Discover specific things that will most effectively communicate your romantic passion for her. Locations, activities, settings, restaurants, vacation spots, romantic overnight getaways. Learn what she loves, and make the sacrifices necessary to bless and romance her. This involves work, gentlemen, even extended effort. It involves planning and budgeting. It is not spontaneous. Even the simplest things require some degree of forethought.

This does not have to be expensive, but it should not be merely practical, either. Giving your wife a DustBuster or a waffle iron might serve or bless her, but it does not qualify as romancing her. We must be quite clear that romancing our wives includes behaviors and activities that are distinctly different from everything else we do in life. As you carefully study your wife, you will be able to move beyond such generalities. You will learn how to romance your wife in ways that are especially meaningful to you as a couple. Those more specific things surely exist, and the sovereign, loving God who joined you to your wife will surely show you what they are.

Romance can be built through phone calls during the workday. I often call Carolyn briefly to say, "I just wanted to hear your voice." It's a small thing that's meaningful to us both. Romance can involve sending letters and notes and, if you are so gifted, even poetry. These should contain carefully composed words that communicate romantic passions. My wife is excellent at this, and I treasure it. In regard to notes, I want to become as thoughtful and forward-thinking as a husband I read about recently:

> When the new car was side-swiped on a trip to the supermarket, Mary Branson stopped and tearfully fumbled in the glove compartment for the insurance papers. Attached to them she found an envelope with her name on it in her husband's handwriting. "Dear Mary," the note said, "When you need these papers, remember it's you I love, not the car."

Romance can be communicated through small gifts. Buying perfume, flowers, and clothing for Carolyn has been a joy for me. As a rule, I despise malls. Shopping is not something I enjoy. But I keep a record of Carolyn's clothing sizes, and I know the three stores in our local mall whose clothing she finds most appealing. Over the years, I have bought her many items from these stores, and what a difference this has made. When I present these gifts to her, I remind her that she is not obligated to keep or wear them, and she knows I mean this. I am thankful that romancing my wife has little to do with my fashion sense, and everything to do with the effort I make to express my feelings for her.

Our date night is my joy, privilege, and responsibility to plan. I maintain a list of fresh ideas by studying the area in which we live, by reviewing magazines and newspapers, and by talking to friends. That way, when Carolyn and I get in the car, I don't have to turn to her and say, "So, uh, where'd you like to eat?" What a joy and what a difference our date night has made in our marriage. It has a definite romantic effect.

Finally, let there be surprises, surprises, surprises. Carolyn lives with a measured anticipation, for she knows that I'm always in the process of creating some sort of romantic surprise for her.

Husbands, there was a time when it was obvious to everyone that you were uniquely passionate about the woman who is now your wife. You couldn't stop thinking about her. You couldn't stop talking about her, or talking to her. You went out of your way to serve and bless her. You spent serious money on her. Is your passion still obvious to those around you? Most importantly, is it still obvious to her?

THE RHYTHM OF LOVE: GOD'S GIFT OF SEX

Where does sexual desire, and the proper means of its fulfillment, come from? We all know the answer: from the mind of God, as part of His plan for man. God created sexual intercourse, as well as the covenant institution that is its proper context. In the beginning, God looked upon the sexual union of husband and wife and saw that it was good. His opinion has not changed in the slightest.

Yet there is within secular culture a perception (which Christianity has largely brought upon itself) that our faith is primarily about sexual prohibitions. Of course, sin has horribly corrupted God's good gift of sex by divorcing it from the covenant of marriage. Accordingly, the misuse of sexuality is flatly condemned in Scripture; the Bible's warnings against immorality and the power of lust must never be denied or ignored. Indeed, even in the Song's unblushing celebration of marriage we find repeated admonitions regarding the proper circumstances of sexual activity (2:7; 3:5; 8:4). But how easy and how common it is to emphasize such biblical prohibitions to the exclusion of the fully God-honoring role of sexuality within marriage. As Duane Garrett has written, "The Bible itself would be incomplete if it only spoke of sexuality in terms of prohibitions and did not give positive instruction to enable the reader to discover the joy of healthy love."[5]

Christians reject all sexual behavior outside of heterosexual marriage, because of God's wise command and because there is indeed something better that lies beyond the wedding reception: a life of sexual intimacy blessed by God, sexual relations within marriage for the purposes of union, pleasure, and procreation. We have thus far seen how the Song of Songs models for us the kind of passionate communication that can and should take place between lovers joined by God in marriage. Of course, there comes a time when the couple must move beyond mere verbal foreplay, as the lovers in Solomon's Song do indeed move.

As this archetypal man and woman enter into lovemaking, they do not hold back, nor does Scripture shrink from recording quite intimate details of their mutually delightful encounter. Indeed, the Song does not limit itself to "who touched who where." Instead, we read of the extravagant indulgence of all five senses. Touch, taste, smell, sight, and hearing are put to full use. Solomon's Song teaches us that lovemaking is intended by God to be an elaborate and pleasurable feast of the senses.

"Your lips drop sweetness as the honeycomb, my bride; milk and honey are under your tongue. The fragrance of your garments is like that of Lebanon" (4:11, NIV). "His mouth is sweetness itself; he is altogether lovely" (5:16, NIV). These two love to kiss one another. They revel in the touch, tastes, and scents associated with their kissing. I would appeal to you to ask your spouse for his or her estimation of your kissing. How does it compare with what is described here?

"Your stature is like that of the palm, and your breasts like clusters of fruit. I said, 'I will climb the palm tree; I will take hold of its fruit.' May your breasts be like the clusters of the vine" (7:7-8, NIV). Sexual touching and caressing of the richest kind are found throughout the Song.

At 4:16, we begin to approach the consummation of this couple's passion on their wedding night. It begins with the woman inviting the man to come and enjoy her love. "Awake, north wind, and come, south wind! Blow on my garden, that its fragrance may spread abroad. Let my lover come into his garden and taste its choice fruits" (NIV).

In 5:1, the man eagerly responds. Again, the poetry is discreet and restrained, yet bursting with passion and completely devoid of vulgarity. "I have come into my garden, my sister, my bride; I have gathered my myrrh with my spice. I have eaten my honeycomb and my honey; I have drunk my wine and my milk" (NIV). Then, at the end of verse 1, we find this ringing affirmation of sexual indulgence within marriage: "Eat, O friends, and drink; drink your fill, O lovers" (NIV). Here, the chorus encourages them both to enjoy lovemaking to the fullest, to be intoxicated with one another in their love. With God as author of Scripture, can there be a clearer expression of the divine approval and encouragement of sexuality within marriage?

Solomon on Setting the Tempo. "He has taken me to the banquet hall, and his banner over me is love" (2:4, NIV). Here is a statement about the intention of the woman's lover, her husband, to make love to her. (See also 4:8 and, in the NASB, 1:4.) In my counseling and pastoring experience, it seems that the husband is more likely than the wife to initiate sexual relations. But in the Song we see that sexual initiative by the wife can in fact be highly appropriate (not to mention, wives, most welcomed by your husband—trust me on that one). The woman portrayed in the Song is not the least hesitant about taking the initiative. In fact, the Song begins with her desiring her lover's kisses and asking him to take her to his bed; and the Song ends with another open request for lovemaking. Her desires are exclusively for her husband, but in the expression of those desires she is, in private, quite uninhibited.

When she says to her man, "Come, my lover, and let us go to the countryside, and let us spend the night in the villages" (7:11), she is not suggesting a shopping trip! She wants him to take her away to a creative location in order to make love to her. This may be the earliest recorded instance of a romantic getaway at a cozy little Bed and Breakfast!

Paul on Picking Up the Beat. In the context of sexual initiative, we must broaden our focus to a portion of the New Testament that speaks to matters of sexual responsiveness. In 1 Corinthians 7:2-4 (NIV), Paul teaches that, no matter which spouse in a marriage takes the sexual initiative, the other partner must be responsive:

> *Since there is so much immorality, each man should have his own wife, and each woman her own husband. The husband should fulfill his marital duty to his wife, and likewise the wife to her husband. The wife's body does not belong to her alone but also to her husband. In the same way, the husband's body does not belong to him alone but also to his wife. Do not deprive each other except by mutual consent and for a time, so that you may devote yourselves to prayer. Then come together again so that Satan will not tempt you because of your lack of self-control.*

Paul's point is clear. The weight is on each spouse's responsibilities and duties, not his or her rights. Most marriages have a history of lovemaking opportunities that have been inappropriately declined. Many of these "No, thank yous" are communicated non-verbally. When they do take verbal form, they often come out something like, "Not tonight, honey. I'm so tired," or, "I'm just not in the mood."

Do such responses violate 1 Corinthians 7:3-4? Surely, many reasons given for depriving a spouse are not biblically acceptable.

Please do not misunderstand. I am not endorsing the imposition of selfish desires on one's spouse under false cover of 1 Corinthians 7. However, while being tired or fatigued are not sinful in themselves, in light of this passage, they cannot be seen as legitimate reasons for depriving a spouse of sexual relations.

What would your response be, ladies, if your husband suggested, "Let's study the Bible together," or "Let's pray together"? Would you reply, "I'm not in the mood"? If he said, "I want to take you to a restaurant this evening," would you say, "I'm sorry, I just don't feel like it"? What if he said, "Can we talk about the children tonight? I'm concerned about some of the behavior I've seen in them lately." Would your first impulse be to reply, "Thanks, honey, but I'm kind of preoccupied right now"?

In other words, ought lovemaking within marriage to be considered a fundamentally spiritual activity (albeit one with potent physical manifestations)? I believe the answer is an unqualified yes.

Proverbs 5:18-19 commands the husband to rejoice with the wife of his youth. Ladies, you must assist your husband in obeying this command. The sexual relationship between husband and wife is to be characterized by rejoicing! Is your sexual relationship joyful? Is it characterized by joy? If not, let me encourage you to discover why not, and don't be satisfied until you do.

Effective lovemaking is not instinctive. If I am living in obedience to 1 Corinthians 7:3-4, I will take my thoughts captive and discipline my body in order to focus primarily on giving to my wife sexually, rather than receiving from her. Indeed, any married person who rightly sees these verses as a directive from God will bring to the marriage bed a servant's mindset that places primary emphasis on the sexual satisfaction of his or her spouse. As one Christian author has wisely written, if you do what comes naturally in lovemaking, almost every time you'll be wrong.

Husbands, are you a skillful and unselfish lover? Don't assume that you know what your wife likes. Don't assume that you know what arouses your wife. Your wife is aroused differently than you are. You must discover what arouses her—and what does not—by engaging her in extended conversation. Gentlemen, we can improve. As lovers, many of us have plateaued, but none have arrived.

Before concluding this section, I want to make some brief points of application.

First, there is the matter of having children in the house. The more children you have, obviously, the more care and planning will be necessary to assure your privacy. Even then, have realistic expectations. Making love will not always be a dynamic experience of sweating and shouting—all the more so if the little ones are just a few feet away on the other side of a bedroom wall, tucked into their bunks but not fully asleep, and possibly wondering why it sounds like Mommy and Daddy are exercising.

Discretion, of course, is necessary. A couple with a sex life that honors God will, over the years, almost certainly be interrupted by children at various inconvenient moments. On many occasions, Carolyn and I have been in our bedroom, door locked, and in the advanced stages of celebrating the gift of sex, when someone knocks gently on the door. Your challenge at that time will be to project a calm tone of voice; it can be quite difficult to sound like you're simply reading a book! If my children were more perceptive, they would realize my vulnerability in those moments.

Knock, knock, knock. "Mom? Dad?"

"Um . . . [clearing of throat, stalling for time]. . . . Yes?"

"Dad, can I have a new car?"

"Uh, sure. . . . Let's talk later."

"Okay, cool. Thanks!"

Second, let me encourage creativity of location in your lovemaking, something illustrated throughout the Song of Songs. On numerous occasions, when Carolyn has picked me up at the airport as I'm coming home from a trip, I've said to her, "Love, I cannot wait to make love to you. See that motel? You and I are paying them a visit." These impromptu times have been romantic and exciting episodes.

Making love is a gift from God, to be done for the glory of God. Husbands, you are not to deprive your wives for any selfish reason. Wives, you are not to deprive your husbands for any selfish reason. If you disagree, please wrestle with 1 Corinthians 7. I believe you will find its teaching far too clear for argument. Even when you are tired and not in the mood, give yourselves to lovemaking that seeks above all to please your spouse, and allow this rich gift of God to unfold in your marriage.

CLOSING THEME: COVENANT LOVE

Of course Solomon's Song is about more than sex. These physical, emotional, and spiritual delights take place in an interpersonal context of covenant commitment. As Carr has noted, "The theme of sexual enjoyment and consummation runs through the book, and the theme of commitment is central to the whole relationship. This is no passing encounter, this is total dedication and permanent obligation."[6]

Look at verses 5-7 of chapter 8 (NIV):

Who is this coming up from the desert leaning on her lover? . . . Place me like a seal over your heart, like a seal on your arm; for love is as strong as death, its jealousy unyielding as the grave. It burns like blazing fire, like a mighty flame. Many waters cannot quench love; rivers cannot wash it away. If one were to give all the wealth of his house for love, it would be utterly scorned.

Here is a dramatic picture of the richness and strength of covenant love:

• She leans on her lover, unashamed to acknowledge publicly her union with him. She and her lover are in covenant, and she wants everyone to know it. It is a defining characteristic of who she and her lover have become: They are two made one, and marked with a seal.

• As death is final, irresistible, and irreversible, so is their covenant love. Their love is jealous with a single-minded passion that leaves room for no other attractions.

• Water in sufficient quantities can smother any flame, but not the flame of this love. Their burning passion is indestructible, of such power and intensity that no river can quench its zeal.

• Their love is beyond value. No price is sufficient to purchase that which is given freely when God joins a man and woman together.

Any attempt at such a purchase would be seen as an act of astonishing crassness, ignorance, and futility.

Such is the power and beauty inherent in every marriage in the Kingdom of God. But we also know that, in this fallen world, love will be tested. Trial and suffering are inevitable for every husband and wife. When you are tempted to consider the attractions of another . . . when a conflict seems difficult to resolve . . . when external challenges test your patience . . . when you have allowed tedium to creep into your life together . . . what will ultimately make the difference? Covenant love.

I close with an excerpt from an editorial published in *Christianity Today:*

> While it comes with clear limits, sex is great. After all, God invented it. . . . The first editors of the King James Version tried to give it a "G" rating by their chapter headings, which suggested that the [Song of Solomon] was not about sex at all, but about Christ and the church. But only a healthy appreciation of sex could lead the biblical writer to remark, with evident pride, that when Moses died at the age of 120, both his eyesight and his "natural force" (which some scholars believe refers to sexual potency) were undiminished. . . . Christians, in other words, are not prudes. We like sex. We celebrate sex. We thank God for sex. But—and here we differ radically with our society—we do not see sex as a right or an end in itself, but as part of discipleship. When we say no to promiscuity or other substitutes for marriage, we do so in defense of good sex. It is not from prudery that the Bible advocates lifelong, faithful, heterosexual marriage, but out of a conviction that the freedom and loving abandon that are necessary for sexual ecstasy come only from a committed marital relationship. . . . Perhaps we ought to make long marriages our image—our "icon"—of sex. An icon is a picture we look to as a model. We study and meditate upon it because it reveals some aspect of God's glory in the world. Our society has made sex its icon. That's why it is found on every magazine stand, in every commercial, every movie aimed at teenagers. This icon portrays only well-curved women and well-muscled young men. It celebrates sex for individual satisfaction.

But look at a couple celebrating their fiftieth wedding anniversary. Let's make them our icon of sex. Their bodies may sag and creak. Their hair is thin or gone. But we see in them something that makes us want to cheer them on. Through them, and only through them and that kind of committed love, shines something of God's glory.[7]

As married couples, let's look forward to a long life together, as we continually learn more about the joys of sexual love within the covenant of marriage. Like the lover and his beloved, let's keep singing Solomon's Song. May we never cease from making that beautiful music, our two voices joined as one in divine harmony, testifying to the world and to one another of the goodness and glory of God.

NOTES

1.   Tom Gledhill, *The Message of the Song of Songs* (Downers Grove, Ill.: InterVarsity, 1994), 23.
2.   G. Lloyd Carr, *The Song of Solomon* (Downers Grove, Ill.: InterVarsity, 1984), 35.
3.   Ibid., 49.
4.   Duane Garrett, *Proverbs, Ecclesiastes, Song of Solomon,* The New American Commentary (Nashville: Broadman, 1993), 379.
5.   Ibid., 367.
6.   Carr, *Song of Solomon,* 53.
7.   William Frey, "Really Good Sex," *Christianity Today* (Aug. 19, 1991), 12.

III

STRATEGIES FOR BUILDING STRONG FAMILIES

6

HOW TO RAISE
MASCULINE SONS[1]

Stu Weber

⸺∞⸺

Helping boys grow into solid men is an enormous ministry opportunity today.

Does that statement sound a bit odd? Doesn't masculinity just happen?

Well, aside from basic physical development, the answer is a resounding no. Maybe in the past our social environment was conducive to a sapling of a boy becoming an oak of a man. But not now. As Garrison Keillor said a few years ago, "Manhood, once an opportunity for achievement, now seems like a problem to be overcome." My own journey provides clues as to what has changed. Most of our sons growing up today would only find a story like mine in a history book or movie about days gone by.

I am in my mid-fifties and grew up in a beautiful little "October Sky" kind of coal mining town in central Washington state. The dads went off to work in the morning and the moms stayed at home. Everybody knew what a man was and a woman was, at least in terms of taking care of and watching out for each other. Divorce was almost nonexistent. The town's residents knew each other. In fact, everybody knew everything, which had its advantages and disadvantages.

Families had dinner together, and television was a novelty and not a life force. For a long time we didn't even have a television set in our home, so on Tuesday nights Dad let us go to the neighbors to watch "Victory at Sea," because World War II was important to him. The rest of the time the family unit was the hub of our lives, and what we learned in school and saw in the community reinforced our family's values. That is how I grew up. I didn't know any other way.

Now that seems like "a long time ago in a galaxy far away." Every little boy knew what every little boy wanted to be, and every little girl knew what every little girl wanted to be. And the distinctions were clearly understood. This was considered normal and okay. We boys, after television became more prevalent, loved a Walt Disney show about Davy Crockett—"king of the wild frontier." We wore little Davy Crockett coonskin hats and took seriously the man's advice: "Be sure you are right, and then go ahead." Our hero's example at the Alamo meant to us that a man should be willing to travel far from home at his own expense, and maybe even at the cost of his life, to help the little people in the world getting the slats kicked out from under their lives. Bottom line, there was a place for strength and a warrior spirit in a man.

But the 1960s changed everything. That decade had many "causes" and "movements," but I believe the one having the greatest influence then, and still expanding now, was "sexual freedom." Attitudes about sexuality and changes in sexual behavior eventually affected everyone. The sexual revolution led to broad tolerance of homosexuality and tampered with core gender definitions and distinctions. Since gender is the base of personal identity, if there is any confusion on basic gender issues there will be confusion on what it means to be a man or woman made in the image of God.

Since this is now such a critical topic, in this chapter I want to try to help church leaders and all Christians understand the basic structure of masculinity and the process of shaping boys into solid men. Of course a similar discussion is needed for girls, but I will leave that for others better suited for the task. The discussion on both topics must occur, though, because the gender issue is, in our day, the very scrimmage line of spiritual warfare.

THE PILLARS OF A MAN'S LIFE

What boys need most is a vision. If boys are going to become men, they need a clear target, a visualization of what a man is. I have found it helpful to describe that manly vision, the infrastructure of masculinity, as the four pillars of a man's heart.

The story of the "first guy," Adam, contains many clues concerning these sturdy columns that buttress manhood. In the Bible's record of Adam's early days, we find that the first man—yet unspoiled by sin—had "pillars" that could bear much weight. They were perfectly straight and balanced. After Adam's miraculous creation, God gave him a place to live and something to do: "Then the Lord God took the man and put him in the Garden of Eden to cultivate it and keep it" (Gen. 2:15, NASB). Adam, still alone, was given a task and responsibility. He wasn't just to hang out and enjoy the place. The garden required someone to "cultivate" and "keep" it. This has not changed. Men still are to take care of things and others, to bear responsibility for providing for those in their care, and to lead. I call this the King Pillar. Of course this quality is not exclusive to the male gender, but I think there is a particular emphasis in masculinity about providing for those who are near and dear.

The second pillar is hinted at in Genesis 2:16-17 (NASB): "And the LORD God commanded the man, saying, 'From any tree of the garden you may eat freely, but from the tree of the knowledge of good and evil you shall not eat.'" Here is a whisper of a man's responsibility to teach and to communicate the way life operates. A man is to know and communicate how life works. I call this the Mentor Pillar. It expresses itself differently by gifting, personality, and temperament, but a man, particularly a father, is called to communicate life wisdom.

A bit further in Adam's story, we find, "for in the day that you eat from it you shall surely die." Here the first man encounters danger. I believe God is implying, "Adam, you need to know that you are vulnerable here. There is a threat in the garden. You could get killed in this place. So be careful." A man may need to fight to keep himself and others safe. He is the man "standing between" his family and all that would harm them. I refer to this as the Warrior Pillar.

Then finally in this passage we read, "Then the LORD God said, 'It is not good for the man to be alone'" (Gen. 2:18). Adam needed help. He needed a companion. A man is made to connect with others. I call this the Friend Pillar. So along came Eve, to complete God's image as male and female. She brought relational genius to the human race. Women generally are much more alert to and adept at relationships than are men. Adam would learn how to relate from Eve. Of course the ultimate attack against aloneness occurs in the magnificent relationship of marriage, but men need help and friendship in every context, whether single or married.

So I see these four "pillars" as a man's core components: the king to provide, the warrior to protect, the mentor to teach, and the friend to connect. These are the qualities we seek to develop in boys who would become mighty men.

The pillars must stand straight and strong, and they must not lean. What are pillars good for if they lean? All they do is fall and crush the people around them. And for too long now, men have been way out of balance and have been crushing people in their imbalance. Let's look at the four pillars, one at a time.

THE KING PILLAR

Jesus is the best example of the qualities revealed by all the pillars, but especially the "King Pillar." Jesus did not order people around, or sit on a throne while servants brought Him grapes and cooled Him by waving palm branches. No, King Jesus—Lord of all—looked out for those in His realm to the point of being willing to die for them. He was the ultimate servant leader, humbling Himself in order to provide for those He loved, treating them as friends and not merely as subjects.

In developing the King Pillar in a boy, you must teach him how a man provides for others both physically and spiritually. Men often understand the need to provide only in terms of the physical well-being of their families—a house, two cars, and an insurance policy. And that is important. One of my sons showed me some evidence of his understanding of this aspect of the King Pillar. He drives a very old pickup truck that my wife and I sold him years ago for one dollar. Now he's married, but he still drives that decaying truck.

"Are you ever going to get a new truck?" I asked him one day.

"No, I am building capital," he answered.

That made me smile. That's a sign of the King Pillar in his life. He and his wife, who is working until children arrive, are saving for the future. They don't spend a nickel of her salary.

But as good as the desire to provide for physical needs is, there is something more important: spiritual provision. A boy needs to accept Jesus Christ. He needs to develop his character in all areas, especially integrity and a good work ethic. He needs to understand and appropriately love the feminine half of the race. All of these qualities are needed to round him out as a king.

A grand king in my life was my grandpa. He would never have used that word to describe himself, for he was "just a coal miner." One time as a young tyke, I was playing a table game with my grandpa and grandma. I didn't want to lose to my grandma, so I cheated. Catching me in the act, Grandpa put his glasses down and said, "Stu, you are a Weber boy, and Weber boys don't lie or cheat or steal."

What an example of a king providing for the spiritual needs of others! Grandpa was looking far into my future and nurturing the health of my soul. In effect he was saying, "You are not just part of the human herd, Grandson. You are a man, and at your core you must have integrity." Such provision is significant in raising a masculine son.

THE WARRIOR PILLAR

In the heart of a man is a desire to protect and even, if necessary, to die for others. In Scripture the warrior is defined as "the man of the in-between."

Think of David in the Valley of Elah. If you want a truly masculine boy, you will say and demonstrate to him, "Son, you stand between trouble and that which would harm those near and dear to you—your wife, your children, your friends, your community."

For some time we have been losing this warrior spirit in our culture. Men have become more passive and tend not to stand "in between" when others are in danger. The young shepherd David was not like that. He walked out to the valley of Elah and said, "What's going on here? The champion of the Philistines is down there every day; but where's the champion of Israel? Who will be the man of the in-between? I'll go down" (1 Samuel 17). And Goliath was soon history.

Centuries later the greatest warrior of all said, "I am the son of David. I will be the man of the in-between. I will stand between my dear ones, my near ones, and all that will destroy them. I will absorb the blows. I will take the wounds. I will shed the blood." And Jesus went to the cross and gave His life so that others would not have to experience eternal death.

One time my boys and I were about to drive away from a drug store when a guy ran out the front door with a package under his arm and the cashier right on his tail, yelling, "Stop, thief!" The boys looked at me, and I looked at them, and we took off after him in our truck. When we stopped the guy, the police arrived minutes later and everything was cool. That's what men do—instinctively and without thinking of all the possible negative consequences—get involved, jump in, stop the trouble.

I am not advocating mindless bravery, of course, or brutish, vicious, unbalanced aggressiveness. I am talking about healthy, self-controlled aggressiveness when this response is needed to protect others. (Hopefully, September 11, 2001, has awakened us to the need for a warrior spirit.) If the Warrior Pillar leans toward passivity, that can hurt people just as much as brutishness. A true warrior is neither a brute nor a coward. A boy needs to be taught the delicate balance between the two extremes.

THE MENTOR PILLAR

The Mentor Pillar concerns wisdom. Every boy needs to learn the role of wisdom in life, not by a parent's lecturing or sermonizing (at least not most of the time) but through patient instruction and, more importantly, modeling.

This is where my dad was so capable. Dad is a quiet, gentle, somewhat "silent type" man of German descent. In his early years he was a coal miner and later he became a city fireman. Although not highly educated in a formal way, he is truly a self-educated man. He spent every spare nickel he had on theology books.

Why was a coal miner and fireman studying theology? My mother wondered. She didn't know the Lord in the early years of their marriage. She couldn't understand Dad's spending all his money on "religious books." But Dad was just so taken with Christ and His Word. He couldn't know enough. So he bought theology books and devoured them. I have a mental snapshot of my father at the dining room table with books spread out. He would have the Bible open and would say, "You guys ought to turn that TV off and look at this." When I would look at the page, it was just a bunch of tiny print. "This is a plan of the ages!" Dad would say excitedly. "The whole world is going to come together like this." The man read the Bible and, because of it, understood life.

Nobody had to tell me I wanted to be like my dad, I just did. He didn't so much mentor by leading formal family devotions. His life was our family devotion.

THE FRIEND PILLAR

The Friend Pillar is the whole bundling of qualities that make a man more sensitive to others. This pillar is probably the most difficult one to build in men. A warrior, for instance, doesn't like a chink in his armor, a place for the knife to go in. That hurts, so many men resist sharing their feelings or "tender side." This cloak of secrecy is destructive to men. A good man needs a tender side to balance his warrior qualities. A wise man is willing to be vulnerable and authentic in the presence of true friends.

Of course, we each have our own hearts and emotions. I did not grow up in an "emotional" home. We shook hands when you did well. And if we were really *overcome* by emotion, our second hand would grab your elbow. But we didn't hug.

I discovered much of my tender side from my youngest boy, Ryan, who taught me to deal with my heart. I was thirty years old when he was born. We had a tuck-in time in our home, which incidentally is a great opportunity to mentor. I always went to the boys' rooms to hang out and say goodnight, and Ryan would always get ahold of me when I would lean down to hug him in bed, and he wouldn't let go. At first it was uncomfortable, and then this little guy said, "Dad, bear hugs are the best." He was right, but the hugging component didn't really compute with me because Ryan was all boy—extremely vigorous, competitive, a capable athlete. Eventually he grew to 6'2" and 220 pounds and was a normal red-blooded guy. But he always had surprising strength in his Friend Pillar. I owe him.

I urge you dads to touch your boys, hug your boys, hold your boys, sit them on your lap, squeeze them. Wrestle with them. And keep up the hugging even when they are older. As they mature, make sure they know that they need to connect with others. Tell them, "Your best friend will be your life partner and you need to learn to connect with her, and with all those who are near and dear to you emotionally. This doesn't come naturally. Work at it. Learn it well."

BUILDING THE PILLARS IN BOYS

How do you build these pillars in the lives of your boys? Here are a few ideas from my own experience.

Read, read, read to your boys. If you don't like to read, get tapes for your boys. Get *The Beginners Bible.* Get *The Chronicles of Narnia.* We still have, in a special "keepsake" place, *The Little Picture Bibles,* with the pages torn to pieces that our kids learned on.

Go outside. When you are developing these pillars in boys, you need a good dose of the out-of-doors. I don't mean you have to be a world-class hunter or fisherman, although those are great sports. Just get outside, maybe just to hike or to go camping or to photograph wildlife. There's something about getting cold and wet and feeling the wind in your face that is good for masculine sons. It's a taste of adversity, and adversity helps us grow.

I remember camping in Oregon's Eagle Cap Wilderness. We were just lying there in the evening, enjoying the magnificent scenery when, all of a sudden, from behind the ridge the storm clouds rolled in. During the night, after a thunderstorm and downpour of rain, the river in our little meadow overflowed its banks and flowed right through the tent. We had to drag the tent up on the hillside in the darkness and try to sleep on a slope in wet sleeping bags. We didn't rest much, but we had a glorious night of learning to face adversity together "in the wild."

Watch good movies. Be discriminating when it comes to the movies you choose, but cinema can communicate messages powerfully. One of the movies we watched years ago when the boys were young was "Chariots of Fire." I had no idea how potent it would become in my son Kent's life. In significant ways it actually shaped the course of his life. He was so stricken with England that he wanted to go there. After graduating from college he went to study at Oxford, where he met a young woman. He later led her to Christ. Still later they married and now have a most magnificent marriage. That's a long way to come, and it all started with that movie when he was a youngster.

Let a boy be a boy. Sometimes this is hard for mothers to understand, especially now that normal masculine traits are suspect among many in our culture. I remember with three sons in our home how many times I had to encourage my wife, Lindy. In rightful exasperation she would say, "We're raising juvenile delinquents!" Having been a boy once, I would respond, "No, they are just boys."

Now, please understand, we were always quick to stop arrogance, disrespect, or dishonesty in their tracks. But roughhousing and wrestling around and having a good time and pulling each other's ears, that was just part of growing up as boys.

There are many more ways to build pillars in a boy's life. Let God guide you. Be creative. Do not neglect to let other men help you, and vice versa. It's good for men and boys to hang out with other godly men and their sons. If you want to be a great basketball player, you have to hang out with great basketball players. If you want to be a good man, you need to hang out with good men. Find some comrades and lock arms with them in training your boys.

The important thing is the vision of manhood: Know what you are after and then dedicate yourself to achieving the goal of building a young man. The concept of the four pillars can help.

The growing process will continue throughout a man's life, and the rewards are significant. My son once came home during his freshman year of college and I could tell he just wasn't himself. This kid was the one who never had a bad day. He was normally jovial, happy-go-lucky, and sweet-hearted. But here he was, depressed and down on himself. I didn't know what to do.

Shared physical activity can provide a good opportunity for a man and his son to talk, so we cleaned the garage. (Now there's a thought—if you're at a loss for what to do, clean the garage!) While tossing boxes, I simply said, "Son, what's happening for you?"

He put down a box. I can still see his muscles rippling in his back, and he turned around and very uncharacteristically said, "I don't know. I don't know anything. Dad, I go to school with guys who have known since they were four years old that they were going to be pediatricians, or rocket scientists, or something. I don't even know what class I'm going to take next term, let alone what I'm going to major in. I feel like I don't know anything."

I heard myself say something completely spontaneous. (Often the best moments are the ones you could never rehearse.) "Well, I don't know either, Son. But I know this—I will be with you."

His head tilted and he said, "You know, Dad, I guess that's all I really need to know right now. Thanks." We then hugged, big time, in the dust and disarray of the garage, and I felt his warm tears on my neck and he felt mine on his. We connected emotionally.

Moments like that change you both for the good. It's all part of becoming a strong, four-pillared man.

So, in raising sons, provide, protect, teach, and connect.

NOTES

1. This chapter is derived from a seminar given by Stu Weber at the "Building Strong Families in Your Church" Conference in Dallas, Texas, in 2000. Bruce Nygren has adapted it here. *Four Pillars of a Man's Heart* by Stu Weber (Sisters, Ore.: Multnomah, 1997) is a full book-length treatment of this subject.

7

HOW TO RAISE FEMININE DAUGHTERS

Susan Hunt

⟨⟩

The very fact that we are asking how to bequeath femininity to our daughters is a sign of the times. We live in a postmodern, relativistic culture that has so thoroughly lost its way that even the simple issue of girls naturally maturing into womanhood is mired in confusion. So how do we approach this topic?

The dictionary defines *feminine* as "belonging to the female sex; characterized by or possessing qualities generally attributed to a woman; womanly."

I could seize that definition and inject it full of the qualities I think should "generally [be] attributed to a woman." I could write a treatise on the obvious effects of feminism and issue a call to women to return to traditional values. I could give a checklist of what good Christian mothers and fathers should be sure their daughters do and don't do. And believe me, I do have opinions! However, a formulaic, prescriptive, behavioral approach is like shifting sand. It may give immediate ideas and temporary solutions, but it will not challenge our daughters to make lasting commitments and changes in the depths of their hearts.

Any discussion of femininity must be driven by God's Word or it will lack substance, integrity, and longevity. I am fully aware of the volatility of this topic, but my primary concern is to present a biblical foundation for womanhood. I believe this positive approach will help us show and tell our daughters the wonders of God's design and calling for women.

One sidebar before we explore this topic: As we think about raising feminine daughters, I encourage you to think covenantally and not just biologically. Our salvation is personal and individual; but when God saves us, He adopts us into His covenant family. We have spiritual brothers, sisters, mothers, and daughters. God deals with us as a household of faith. Whether or not we have biological daughters, we have spiritual daughters, and it is our covenant privilege and responsibility to pass on a legacy of biblical womanhood to those girls and young women entrusted to our church.

Now let's explore a biblical foundation for womanhood.

PURPOSE AND AUTHORITY

Whenever we craft a biblical apologetic for any topic, we need to begin by putting that topic in the larger context of creation, fall, and redemption. If we simply lift a few Scripture verses out of context and use those verses to construct our apologetic, we will likely come away with distortions. The same is true for womanhood. Our starting point is not roles and behaviors. The fundamental question is: What is our purpose and authority? Creation, fall, and redemption give the answers.

The opening words of Scripture tell us that "In the beginning God created the heavens and the earth. . . . God said, 'Let there be light,' and there was light" (Gen. 1:1, 3, NIV).

God is the Creator. He spoke, and creation happened. His Word is the absolute authority.

On the sixth day of creation God said, "Let us make man in our image, in our likeness, and let them rule over the fish of the sea and the birds of the air, over the livestock, over all the earth, and over all the creatures that move along the ground" (Gen. 1:26, NIV).

It is incredible that the God whose words brought creation into existence would make a creature in His own image. The Creator

King fashioned a creature who would mirror certain aspects of His own character. This is what would set this creature apart from all the others.

> *So God created man in his own image, in the image of God he created him; male and female he created them.*
> —GEN. 1:27, NIV

The man and the woman were created with the capacity to reflect the very character of God. Herein lies the purpose and dignity of humankind.

Purpose and authority are the first steps in building a biblical worldview, including our perspective of womanhood. *The Westminster Shorter Catechism* underscores this by beginning with these two foundational questions:

> Q. 1. What is the chief end of man?
> A. Man's chief end is to glorify God and to enjoy Him forever.
> Q. 2. What rule hath God given to direct us how we may glorify and enjoy Him?
> A. The word of God, which is contained in the Scriptures of the Old and New Testaments, is the only rule to direct us how we may glorify and enjoy Him.[1]

Our purpose is God's glory, and our authority to know how to glorify Him is His Word. This shapes and simplifies life.

But the first man and woman rebelled against God's authority. Adam and Eve chose self-governance rather than God's rule. Sin separated them from God and from the reason for their existence. They could no longer live in God's presence, and so they could no longer reflect His glory. Adam was our representative; so his fallen nature and the wretched consequences of his sin were passed on to the human race.

But God did not leave us in this predicament. Through the covenant of grace, God made the way for us to be redeemed from sin and to live in His presence. In this covenant, Christ is our representative. He kept the terms of the covenant for us. He lived a perfectly obedient life and offered Himself as the payment for our sin. God's covenant promise is, "I will give them a heart to know me, that I am the LORD. They will be my people, and I will be their God" (Jer. 24:7, NIV). We do not deserve salvation, and we can do nothing to earn it. It is glorious grace from beginning to end.

SOME PRACTICAL IMPLICATIONS OF PURPOSE AND AUTHORITY

Our daughters will be products of their theology. Their knowledge— or lack of knowledge—of who God is and what He has done for them will show up in every attitude, action, and relationship. Their world-view will be determined by their belief system.

We must teach our daughters that their value and identity lie in the fact that they are image-bearers of the God of glory. This will protect them from seeking significance in the inconsequential shallowness of self-fulfillment, personal happiness, materialism, or others' approval.

Our daughters must know the wondrous truth that their overarching purpose in life is God's glory. This must determine every decision they make, from their choice of clothes to their choice of a husband. The question that guides all of our decisions should be: Does this glorify God? First Corinthians 10:31 should be one of the first verses they memorize: "So whether you eat or drink or whatever you do, do it all for the glory of God." And they should see us making decisions based on this mandate.

The world will tempt our daughters to look to their feelings and experiences as their authority, but we must show and tell them that God's Word is the ultimate authority for faith and life.

We must tell our daughters about the expanse of God's love. They must know that we are justified and sanctified by grace. It seems that women are particularly prone to a performance orientation of life. We may acknowledge that we are saved by grace, but somehow we get entangled in "works righteousness" when we it comes to our sanctification. We think that if we are a little better, God will love us a little more. This distortion spills over into all other relationships. *If I'm a little better, my parents will love me more . . . or my friends will love me more*

. . . or my husband will love me more. This is exhausting for the one trying to earn everyone's love, and it drains the people whose approval we are trying to earn. Children who think they must establish their own righteousness through accepted behavior eventually become so weary that they give up or become masters of deceit.

A biblical understanding of justification will free our daughters. The more they understand that God declares us to be just in His sight on the basis of the finished work of Jesus Christ, and that the righteousness of Jesus is deposited in our spiritual bank accounts, the more they will live in the beauty and freedom of His grace.

All of this means that I must search my own heart. Am I trying to elevate myself through my daughter's accomplishments and behavior? Is my primary concern her happiness or her holiness? Is God's glory really the driving passion of my own life? These questions take me to the cross. They take me to Jesus to plead for grace and wisdom.

It is against this backdrop that we are able to perceive the particular uniqueness of God's creation of woman.

WOMAN'S CREATION DESIGN

In Genesis 2 we read, "The LORD God said, 'It is not good for the man to be alone. I will make a helper suitable for him'" (v. 18, NIV).

Why was it "not good for the man to be alone"? Because he was created in the image of the Triune God. The unity and diversity of the Trinity demanded an image-bearer that reflected this equal-but-different characteristic.

Equality did not preclude gender distinctiveness; rather, equality allowed the distinctiveness of the man and the woman to be so perfectly complementary that it blended into a mysterious oneness that gloriously reflected the oneness of the Trinity.

The helper design of the woman brought a completeness to the garden home that received God's pronouncement, "It is very good."

Yet we live in a culture whose hostility against this design and order has raged for several decades. The feminist philosophy says that equality means sameness and insists on independence from husbands and family. Now the daughters of those feminists are confused.

In her book *What Our Mothers Didn't Tell Us,* Danielle Crittenden writes:

> For in all the ripping down of barriers that has taken place over a generation, we may have inadvertently also smashed the foundations necessary for our happiness. Pretending that we are the same as men—with similar needs and desires—has only led many of us to find out, brutally, how different we really are. In demanding radical independence—from men, from our families—we may have also abandoned certain bargains and institutions that didn't always work perfectly but until very recently were civilization's best ways of taming the feckless human heart.[2]

Crittenden's research and analysis are helpful, but her solutions are flawed because they begin with woman and not with God. She, too, is searching for what will make women happy, and it is an endless journey.

I pray that our daughters will write books entitled "What Our Mothers Told Us" and that these books will celebrate God's creation purpose and His design of woman. This is a design that is never outdated because it transcends time and place. It is bigger than any given role in life, but it impacts every role. It is the design stamped upon us at creation. It is intrinsic to who we are as women.

So, let's explore this helper design. In the Old Testament the Hebrew word for *helper* is used primarily to refer to God as our Helper. When we consider how God is our Helper, we begin to see the richness and strength of this word.

Moses spoke of God as his Helper who saved him from the sword of Pharaoh (Ex. 18:4).

In Psalms we read that God is the Helper of the victim, the fatherless, the needy, and the afflicted (Ps. 10:14; 72:12; 86:17).

God is referred to as our Helper who is our support, strength, and shield (Ps. 20:2; 28:7; 33:20).

I think you get the picture. This is not a fragile word, and we are not called to a mission of fluff. Our helper ministry is one of defense, comfort, and compassion. I addressed this topic in my book *By Design:*

The helper design is multi-dimensional. Different women will exhibit different aspects of this design in various ways. The same woman may exhibit it differently in each season of her life.... The relational strength of our helper design causes women to attach fiercely to people and purposes. We don't turn loose easily. This tenacity equips women to persevere in intercessory prayer for years. Countless mothers have prayed for wayward children long after others lost hope....

We live in a culture void of hope. Woman's helper design uniquely qualifies us to enter this vacuum and to give help by proclaiming the "Hope of Israel, its Savior in times of distress" (Jer. 14:8).

In Psalm 146, the words *help* (*'ēzer*) and *hope* are linked together. This is significant. Help apart from hope is superficial and temporary. It is merely a stopgap measure that is a substitute for the real thing. Yet this is what our culture offers....

The woman who can give authentic help is the one who has come to a place of hopelessness in self that drives her to God's Word where she finds her "help is the God of Jacob," and her "hope is in the Lord." She is qualified to help others because she has an eternal relationship with the Lord and she is saturated with His Word. She points them to the only viable Object of hope by directing them to the only veritable Source of hope. This is authentic help.[3]

Sin marred that design, and now woman tries to reinvent womanhood on her own terms. Since Satan slithered into the garden and convinced Eve to try the way of independence and individualism, women have been on a quest for their own happiness. In this autonomous vacuum the helper design is senseless and useless.

It is because of our redemption that we *can* live out our helper design. It is our redemption that breaks the reign of sin in our lives and empowers us to fulfill our creation mission. And it is our knowledge of our Redeemer's love for us that compels us to do so. In the covenant community, the helper design makes sense. Two of the characteristics of covenant life are community and compassion, and this is exactly what our helper design equips us to cultivate. Our nurturing and relational strengths prepare us to foster a sense of family in the home and church and to be channels of compassion to the victims, fatherless, needy, and afflicted.

SOME PRACTICAL IMPLICATIONS OF THE HELPER DESIGN

The redeemed woman who has a biblical apologetic of womanhood has a focus and clarity of purpose that enables her to be a true helper. She will embrace her helper design and will encourage and equip her daughters to do the same.

The redeemed helper will be a woman of prayer. She will defend her family and the covenant family on her knees, and her daughters will be drawn to emulate her selfless strength.

The redeemed helper whose covenant sensibilities have been honed understands the importance of the virtue of domesticity and the ministry of hospitality. But she knows this is more than baking her own bread and having a beautifully decorated home. Domesticity means a devotion to home life. It seems to me that the most definitive statement of domesticity was made by Jesus when He said, "Do not let your hearts be troubled. . . . In my father's house are many rooms. . . . I am going there to prepare a place for you" (John 14:1-2, NIV).

Domesticity means that we prepare safe places where troubled hearts can find rest and comfort, and we involve our daughters in this ministry in our homes and in our churches. In a must-read book for every woman, nineteenth-century pastor John Angell James said, "Whatever breaks down the modest reserve, the domestic virtues, the persuasive gentleness, of woman, is an injury done to the community."[4]

The redeemed helper is not inward-focused. You will find her taking her children to visit the elderly as well as taking them across social and cultural barriers to extend the boundaries of the covenant to the oppressed and needy and afflicted. And as she does so, she trains another generation to live covenantally.

The redeemed helper who is not married understands that she is to be a mother in Israel and that she is to join with other women to be corporate helpers in God's covenant community.

The redeemed helper values male and female distinctiveness because she knows that this is God's design and order. She is not threatened by male headship. She knows that submission has nothing to do with status. Submission has to do with function. It is the way God has ordered life in the kingdom, and it is good because He is good. This is a reflection of the ontological equality yet the functional difference in the Trinity. Headship and submission are God's ordained means for achieving oneness in marriage. She knows that submission is not a legalistic list of behaviors or mindless passivity. She understands that it is not about logic; it is about love. It defies logic that Jesus would release all the glories of heaven so that He could give us the glory of heaven. In Philippians we are told:

> *Your attitude should be the same as that of Christ Jesus: Who, being in very nature God, did not consider equality with God something to be grasped, but made himself nothing, taking the very nature of a servant, being made in human likeness. And being found in appearance as a man, he humbled himself and became obedient to death—even death on a cross!*
> —PHIL. 2:5-8, NIV

Jesus loved us so much that He voluntarily submitted to death on a cross. His command is that wives are to submit to their husbands. This is a gift that we voluntarily give to the man we have vowed to love, in obedience to the Savior we love. The redeemed helper knows that submission does not restrict her—it actually frees her to fulfill her helper design. And as she lives in the light of this truth, her daughters watch and learn. Quoting again from *By Design:*

> There is an interesting verse in Psalm 144: " . . . our daughters will be like pillars carved to adorn a palace" (Psalm 144:12).
>
> A pillar, according to the dictionary, is "a . . . support; one who occupies a central or responsible position." Some of the meanings of the root Hebrew word that is used here are: "to attend, to defend, to give stability, to join." The ideas of protection and support are clear in this imagery.
>
> In summary, a helper supports by protecting, sustaining, upholding, refreshing, attending, defending, and stabilizing.[5]

HOW DO WE PASS THE LEGACY OF BIBLICAL WOMANHOOD TO OUR DAUGHTERS?

This is certainly not an exhaustive list of suggestions, but at least it will get us started.

First, we must remember that God has given us every resource we need. He has given us His Holy Spirit. We have the very power of God within us to give us grace and wisdom for the task, and we must pray for this same power to be at work in our daughters. It is the power of the gospel that will transform them.

> *I am not ashamed of the gospel, because it is the power of God for the salvation of everyone who believes.*
>
> —ROM. 1:16, NIV

> *And we, who with unveiled faces all reflect the Lord's glory, are being transformed into his likeness with ever-increasing glory, which comes from the Lord, who is the Spirit.*
>
> —2 COR. 3:18, NIV

He has given us His Word. We must diligently teach our daughters biblical truth and pray that the Holy Spirit will apply that truth to their hearts.

> *How can a young man [or woman] keep his [or her] way pure? By living according to your word. . . . I have hidden your word in my heart that I might not sin against you.*
>
> —PS. 119:9, 11, NIV

God has given us the privilege of prayer. We should pray for hedges of protection around our daughters. Select portions of Scripture and pray them into your daughter's life. For example, pray that she will trust in the Lord with all her heart and never lean on her own understanding; that in all her ways she will acknowledge Him, for He will make her paths straight. Pray that she will not be wise in her own eyes, but that she will fear the Lord and shun evil (Prov. 3:5-7). Pray Proverbs 31 for her.

The Lord has given us the church. The covenant family is part of our inheritance as members of the family of God. The church is "the pillar and foundation of the truth" (1 Tim. 3:15, NIV), and believing parents have the unrivaled resource of the teaching and the relationships provided there. Louis Berkhof wrote:

> Now, the children of the covenant are adopted into a family that is infinitely higher than the family of any man of rank or nobility. They are adopted into the family of the covenant God Himself. Even while on earth they are privileged to join the company of the redeemed, the saints of God. They take their place in the church of Jesus Christ, which is the heavenly Jerusalem.[6]

When our daughters are taught the truth of biblical womanhood, and they see the wonder and substance of this reality being lived out among Christian women, I believe they will be dazzled and will flourish.

> *The righteous will flourish like a palm tree, they will grow like a cedar of Lebanon; planted in the house of the LORD, they will flourish in the courts of our God. They will still bear fruit in old age, they will stay fresh and green, proclaiming, "The LORD is upright; he is my Rock, and there is no wickedness in him."*
>
> —Ps. 92:12-15, NIV

Second, the fight to recapture biblical womanhood is a spiritual battle, and we must utilize every weapon God has provided as we engage in this conflict. We cannot deny the fact that we have breathed feminist air for several decades. This poison has taken its toll. Raising daughters who are committed to a biblical perspective of womanhood will be like standing against a tidal wave. But stand we must.

> *Finally, be strong in the Lord and in his mighty power. Put on the full armor of God so that you can take your stand against the devil's schemes. For our struggle is not against flesh and blood, but against the rulers, against the authorities, against the powers of this dark world and*

against the spiritual forces of evil in the heavenly realms. Therefore put
on the full armor of God, so that when the day of evil comes, you may
be able to stand your ground, and after you have done everything, to
stand.

—EPH. 6:10-13, NIV

Third, we must teach our daughters that living for God's glory is
beyond their ability. It is a work of grace. We should teach them to flee
to the cross for grace and mercy, and then to become a stream of grace
and mercy to others. They will learn this best by seeing us live in this
way.

Fourth, we must teach our daughters about biblical womanhood
as we "sit at home and when [we] walk along the road, when [we] lie
down and when [we] get up" (Deut. 6:7, NIV). We are teaching a way
of life as we live life.

John Angell James, the nineteenth-century pastor quoted earlier,
wrote about teaching our children through the course of everyday circumstances:

> It is the sentiments you let drop occasionally, it is the conversation
> they overhear, when playing in the corner of the room, which has
> more effect than many things which are addressed to them
> directly. . . . Your example will educate them—your conversation
> with your friends—the business they see you transact—the likings
> and dislikings you express—these will educate them. . . . The edu-
> cation of circumstances . . . is of more constant and powerful
> effect, and of far more consequence to the habit, than that which
> is direct and apparent. This education goes on at every instant of
> time; it goes on like time—you can neither stop it nor turn its
> course.[7]

Fifth, we must not be naïve. We must be wise, like the "men of
Issachar, who understood the times and knew what Israel should do"
(1 Chron. 12:32, NIV). We must be aware of cultural influences, and
we must warn our daughters of the dangers of ungodliness.

What kind of women will it take to raise feminine daughters? It
will take true women.

The True Woman

In a book by this title I give the following explanation:

> The dictionary defines *true* as "consistent with fact or reality; exactly conforming to a rule, standard, or pattern." . . .
>
> The true woman is the real thing. She is a genuine, authentic Masterpiece. The Master has set eternity in her heart and is conforming her to His own image. There is consistency in her outward behavior because it is dictated by the reality of her inner life. That reality is her redemption.
>
> The true woman is a reflection of her redemption. . . .
>
> By the transforming power of the Gospel, the Christian woman is empowered by God's Spirit to give an increasingly true reflection of her Savior and thus to be a true woman. . . .
>
> When my friend Sharon Kraemer was diagnosed with cancer, her response was, "I am confident that God will use this to take me deeper into His love for me." I didn't see Sharon until several weeks after surgery and several rounds of chemotherapy, and at my first sight of her I gasped. It was not because her body and her hair were so thin. My shock was because Sharon absolutely glowed with peace and love. She was awash with an undeniable radiance. I could only exclaim, "Sharon, you must have been spending some incredible times with the Lord." She did not need to reply. The evidence was there.
>
> This is the essence of the true woman. Regardless of the time in history when she inhabits this earth, she is one who lives in the presence of glory. Her redeemed character is shaped and driven by God's Word and Spirit. Because she is the very dwelling-place of the Lord God, her reflection of Him is manifested in every relationship and circumstance of life. The distinguishing characteristic of her life is His presence in her radiating out to all who see her. The true woman's life is not segmented into sacred and secular. All of life is sacred because it is lived in His presence. The true woman is a true reflection of God's glory.[8]

Recently our granddaughter, Mary Kate, made her public profession of faith and was received as a full communing member of her church. Three generations of women in our family sat together and watched the fourth generation pledge herself to Jesus Christ as each of us had done. There was a rush of gratitude for God's covenant faithfulness to families, and a profound sense of our responsibility to pass on a legacy of biblical womanhood. Mary Kate, and the generation of covenant daughters she represents, does not foresee the battles to be fought. But, to some degree, we know. And we are covenant-bound to "train the younger women . . . set them an example by doing what is good . . . while we wait for the blessed hope—the glorious appearing of our great God and Savior, Jesus Christ, who gave himself for us to redeem us from all wickedness and to purify for himself a people that are his very own, eager to do what is good" (Titus 2:4, 7, 13-14, NIV).

May God give us grace and wisdom, and may He be pleased to give us daughters who have a passion to live for and to reflect His glory.

NOTES

1. *The Westminster Confession of Faith, Together with the Larger Catechism and the Shorter Catechism* (Atlanta: Presbyterian Church in America Committee for Christian Education & Publications, 1990).

2. Danielle Crittenden, *What Our Mothers Didn't Tell Us* (New York: Simon & Schuster, 1999), 25.

3. Susan Hunt, *By Design* (Wheaton, Ill.: Crossway, 1994), 101, 108, 171, 173.

4. John Angell James, *Female Piety* (London: Hamilton Adams, 1860; reprinted Morgan, Pa.: Soli Deo Gloria, 1994), 75.

5. Hunt, *By Design,* 118.

6. Louis Berkhof and Cornelius Van Til, *Foundations of Christian Education: Addresses to Christian Teachers,* ed. Dennis E. Johnson (Phillipsburg, N.J.: Presbyterian and Reformed, 1990; originally published Grand Rapids, Mich.: Eerdmans, 1953), 77.

7. John Angell James, *A Help to Domestic Happiness* (London: Frederick Westley and A. H. Davis, 1833; reprinted Morgan, Pa.: Soli Deo Gloria, 1995), 128-129.

8. Susan Hunt, *The True Woman* (Wheaton, Ill.: Crossway, 1997), 22, 34-35.

8

The TALKS Mentoring Curriculum and Approach

Harold D. Davis

※

For years I have been actively involved in helping children. I'm also a preacher, and one of my favorite scriptures is James 1:27 (KJV): "Pure religion and undefiled before God and the Father is this: to visit the fatherless and widows in their affliction, and to keep oneself unspotted from the world."

I believe every young person needs a mature adult willing to challenge him or her with wisdom in the context of love. I was fortunate to have a dad who would tell me from time to time, "Boy, you're crazy!" When I thought about it, he was right. I was crazy. Most fifteen- and sixteen-year-old boys are crazy, and they need a man in their face challenging them with superior wisdom.

To us Christians, James 1:27 is a call not just to religion in general but to put our faith into action by looking after fatherless young people. In my city a few years ago, a community symposium was held where local leaders talked about the needs of our youth. The keynote speaker, Donald Draayer, had been an educator for thirty-nine years and was once National School Superintendent of the Year. After offering some suggestions toward improving our youth programs, he said, "The best solutions are those created locally. . . . [The] key in any event is for adults to connect with kids on an individual basis. . . .

The only way to develop assets is to have relationships, kids talking with older folks and older folks talking with kids."[1] Draayer made me feel good, because the TALKS (Transferring A Little Knowledge Systematically) mentoring approach and curriculum is just that: a systemized way for adults to connect and share wisdom with young people.

As a parent and youth worker, I am surrounded by kids. At times I forget that my experience is not the norm. Many adults have little to no interaction with young boys and girls. A man may take a boy out for pizza, to a baseball game, or just to hang out, but he probably won't do it on a regular basis—systematically. Our society has a television mentality where everything is resolved in a half-hour minus commercials, but the solutions we need to youth problems will not happen overnight. Nothing will change the negative direction that many of our young people are going in until we get adults and kids around the table for the purpose of regular, meaningful dialogue. This is the focus of the TALKS curriculum and approach.

This is the thesis statements for TALKS:

> Every boy needs a man in his face who will challenge him with wisdom regarding the critical issues and decisions in his life.

> Every girl needs a woman in her world who will challenge her with wisdom regarding the critical issues and decisions in her life.

I often encounter middle school boys who think they know more than I do. I love to sit them down, let them make their statements, and then very methodically take the legs out from under their arguments. Often they have nothing more to say. They are not accustomed to having a man bump heads with them intellectually, particularly if they have been raised by a mother or grandmother. In a society where youth are not regularly exposed to the wisdom of more experienced adults, young people as they make decisions must pull from their own knowledge and limited experience. Americans don't have rites of passage in the same sense that other cultures do. We just let kids grow up. Without a network of caring adults in their lives, or even one meaningful relationship with a loving, mature adult, boys and girls are left to determine life's flow and meaning from their peer group.

It is a terrible thing to live in the United States of America and have no personal "advocate" to help you. As I go into our school systems and observe young people in trouble, I see that those without advocates move swiftly through the system and toward incarceration. God is very concerned with the helpless in our society. Remember James 1:27 (see also Isa. 1:17, 19, 23; Job 29:12; 1 John 3:17).

Even kids who are not considered "at-risk" benefit greatly from a variety of adult advocates in their lives. How much real dialogue is happening between generations in the average American family? I know wonderful fathers who neglect to teach specific things to their kids. I have a wonderful son and we have a wonderful relationship. Yet when I am teaching concepts to my "mentees," I'll find myself thinking, *Did I teach my son about this?*

I believe that the church of Jesus Christ should stand up when the home fails, and be next in line to deal with problems. I don't blame the schools. Instead, I see a wide-open door of opportunity for the church, and in some capacities, the schools are asking churches for help.

Concerning the separation of church and state, Christians should have the same right as any other group to go into the schools, not to promote our religious beliefs but to help! The majority of our TALKS mentors are committed Christians. We go into the schools, not preaching Jesus, but *living* Jesus and letting our actions speak.

THE TALKS MOVEMENT

TALKS is a grass-roots mentoring movement. It takes only one individual to get it started in a given locality. In my city I mentored three boys by myself. Then seven of my friends joined me, and together we mentored twenty-one boys. Three years later we had around eighty mentors, both men and women, helping almost 250 children.

This is happening in cities around the country. You may have noticed the growing trend in our country for adults to try to reach children through mentoring. Because this is something I have done naturally in the past, I devised a structure where other people could do it also, regardless of their areas of giftedness.

When beginning a mentoring program, it is very important to have a strategy and structure in place. When devising the strategy for my city, I asked the following questions: How do I get adults and children talking? Which level(s) of mentoring will I address? How will mentors and mentees spend their time together? What will they talk about?

The TALKS approach to mentoring answers these questions through three strategic components:

• Strategy 1: Minimum mentoring. Mentors keep a one-hour-per-week time commitment (a businesslike relationship with the children).

• Strategy 2: One adult mentoring three children.

• Strategy 3: The use of an issue-oriented curriculum based on applying wisdom to daily life.

Strategy 1: Minimum Mentoring

The TALKS mentoring movement focuses on "minimum mentoring," a preventive strategy for helping large numbers of youth while providing a simple structure for busy working adults to maximize the time that they spend with the mentees. (Chapter 9 will describe other levels of TALKS mentoring, in the context of men mentoring boys—my own area of greatest expertise.) All mentoring takes place at the school during the school day, and generally employers are willing to give their employees one hour per week of leave time from the job to do the mentoring.

Our mentors spend just thirty minutes a week with each mentee. No evenings, weekends, extended hours, trips, or the like. This level of mentoring is not for "hard-core" kids. But if we can get such a program flourishing, we'll have fewer hard-core kids.

We begin our mentoring groups at the elementary school level and have the mentor follow the children through each grade. Over a period of years, the thirty minutes a week of sharing wisdom can have a tremendous influence on the young people. At the same time the mentors do not get burned out and are able to give more time in the long run.

Another form of protection for the mentor and the mentee that is built into the TALKS approach is the expectation of maintaining a businesslike relationship between the adults and the children. To introduce this concept, we begin the mentoring relationship with a "contract-signing ceremony." (See the following illustrations of sample contracts.)

Mentor's Contract

(To Be Completed and Given to the Student)

I _____

make this contract with my student

_____

to participate in this program with good intentions.

I will read the chapters and participate in the weekly sessions.

I will genuinely and respectfully consider what my student shares with me but will also feel free to express my opinions.

I will not share other people's private information outside of our cell group.

I also understand that my student has a busy schedule just like mine and there may be times when it will be necessary to reschedule.

I will be understanding when this happens.

I will view this interaction as an opportunity to share wisdom which will benefit my student for years to come.

"How much better is wisdom than gold, and understanding than silver!"

—King Solomon

_____

Mentor's Signature

_____

Student's Signature

_____

Witness

_____

Date

STUDENT'S CONTRACT

(To Be Completed and Given to the Mentor)

I _____

make this contract with my mentor

_____

to participate in this program with good intentions.

I will read the chapters and participate in the weekly sessions.

I will genuinely and respectfully consider what my mentor shares with me but will also feel free to express my opinions.

I will not share other people's private information outside of our cell group.

I also understand that my mentor has a busy schedule just like mine and there may be times when it will be necessary to reschedule. I will be understanding when this happens.

I will view this interaction as an opportunity to share wisdom which will benefit me for years to come.

"How much better is wisdom than gold,
and understanding than silver!"

—KING SOLOMON

_____

Student's Signature

_____

Mentor's Signature

_____

Witness

_____

Date

To begin the ceremony, a TALKS representative introduces the mentors to the students and explains that the mentors are volunteering their time to come to the school and share wisdom with them. We tell the students that they have been selected to participate in this leadership program and that there are a series of expectations that they must adhere to. (If we tell the students it is a mentoring program, they wonder, "What did I do? Did I do something wrong?" And in a couple of instances, a parent inquired as to why her child was selected to be a part of the "mentoring program." We avoid attaching a stigma to the children; TALKS is not a "remedial" program. In actuality, many parents have called us and asked if their child could have a mentor.)

Once the students understand that they will be meeting to "conduct the business of wisdom" with the adult mentor, we talk through the contract. We basically preach and teach each clause. For example: "To participate with good intentions means you will not come with an attitude. Mr. Johnson is busy. He takes off work to come over here to be with you. Do you promise you will have a good attitude?" After they agree, each student initials the clause and we move on.

One of my favorite statements in the contract is: "I will genuinely and respectfully consider what my mentor shares with me, but will also feel free to express my opinions." I take this opportunity to teach the children how to disagree politely with adults. We help each child memorize this sentence: "Mr. Smith, I would like to respectfully disagree with you." I encourage them to practice using this sentence on their mentor, teachers, principal, mom, and other adults. After everyone signs the contracts, the mentors keep them and refer back to them from time to time to remind the kids of their commitment.

During the course of mentoring, I give our mentors permission to send any child back to the classroom if the child is not keeping his or her end of the contract. If there are any recurring problems with the child's behavior, a TALKS representative will visit the mentoring cell and refer back to the original contract. We ask the unwilling students if they want to keep the contract or stop meeting with the mentor. Most of the time they do want to continue and will change their behavior, but there may be instances when they will quit or we will move them to a different mentoring cell.

Remember, this is minimum-level mentoring. Everyone understands that the purpose of getting together is to discuss wisdom. I tell the children up front that this is not about fun; this is about business.

I ask them, "Can you hang with that? Are you mature enough to do that, or do I need to go to the higher grade and get somebody more mature?"

Always they answer, "No, we can do it. We can do it."

I continually remind the mentors to keep a businesslike atmosphere for their own health. Generally, in mentoring programs where children have unrestrained access to adults, the mentors burn out and will not mentor again. The interesting thing about TALKS is that we don't lose mentors to burnout. I strongly discourage "minimum" mentors from spending more than the thirty minutes per week of contact time with the children. Many of them think they can do more, but the truth is, they do not have the emotional reserves or the energy. Women, especially, tend to want to get more involved, but the TALKS approach was designed for soft-level mentoring. If a mentor has to quit, we put another mentor in his place. If a child moves or drops out, we put another child in the group. It's like business.

Strategy 2: One Adult Mentoring Three Children

The TALKS approach also uses a one-adult-with-three-children model for mentoring. There are some advantages to having one adult meet with three children.

First, it provides a way to multiply the effort. It is too late in our society to get the job done with only one-on-one mentoring. Too many children need our help and too many adults are hiding behind their busy schedules and not dealing with the issue. Second, one adult meeting with three children creates a group dynamic for interaction. We try to place a variety of personalities in the group, such as one wonderful child, one who is challenging, and one who is in the middle. They may have different academic or social abilities and cultural or racial backgrounds.

This approach discourages manipulation and unhealthy bonding. For example, many mentors who mentor a child one-on-one get manipulated by the child. A streetwise kid can manipulate an adult if the mentor is not a trained educator, psychologist, or seasoned parent. It is more difficult for one boy or girl to get away with manipulation when two others are present. Likewise, when a mentor meets with three mentees, no one child can expect all of the attention. Most men are "maxed out" already with family, job, and other responsibilities. When they spend time with a boy, the boy may latch on, seeing the mentor as a "daddy-replacement." This can frighten men and cause them to shy away from mentoring, since this goes beyond the boundaries of "soft-level" mentoring. But in a mentoring cell of three boys, they look around the table and see that the mentor can't be everyone's daddy, and they do not burden the mentor with unrealistic expectations.

There is also a sifting or screening process in the one-with-three model. If I give you just one mentee, maybe your personalities will click right away and you will get off to a great start. But there is the chance that you will spend a great deal of time just establishing rapport with the young person only to find that your personalities do not match too well, or that the child is not able to receive what you are offering. With three mentees, the odds increase that your mentoring experience will begin well and remain positive. In a group where one child is very eager to see you, one is more neutral, and one is harder to reach, your positive outlook combined with the positive child and the child who could go either way will put positive peer pressure on the third child to be a key part of the group.

In my own mentoring cell, I met with the same three boys when they were in third grade, fourth grade, and fifth grade. When they went to three different middle schools, the group had to split up, so I chose the boy that I felt I would benefit the most and have the most influence on and created a new mentoring cell with him and two other boys at his new school.

In my city we have mentors at all levels—elementary school, middle school, and high school. I prefer to begin mentors with kids in elementary school and have them follow the kids through each grade level. Every school has a different personality, a different flavor. Elementary schools are often more flexible and willing to accommodate mentors' schedules. In middle school the students adhere to a stricter schedule and mentors may come only during certain periods.

We work closely with the principal or school counselor, social worker, teachers, secretaries, or appointed school staff to create the mentor cells and align them with the mentor's schedule.

Strategy 3: Issue-oriented Curriculum

The TALKS curriculum was designed to help average adults communicate effectively with young people about relevant issues. You don't have to be a seasoned expert in working with youth or a trained teacher to use this curriculum, which consists of student texts and mentor guides for male mentors and boys ("Talks My Father Never Had with Me") and student texts and mentor guides for female mentors and girls ("Talks My Mother Never Had with Me").

These are issue-oriented guides. Each chapter deals with a separate topic. One advantage of using such a text is that the book is the "villain." The text itself is the bad guy when you are reading it with the children. Eventually, something will come up that each student doesn't like. No one can say that the mentor is picking on them if you start in chapter 1 and proceed systematically. The text makes it easier to discuss hard issues, because the children feel free to disagree with the author, which frees and enlivens the dialogue. And the mentor is free to share his or her opinion without stifling further conversation on the matter.

The TALKS mentoring movement is intended to address the needs of all children as they grow to adolescence and young adulthood. We emphasize their leadership potential, focusing on the mentoring time as an opportunity to gain wisdom and skills that will benefit them for years to come.

I occasionally get letters that share how the TALKS program has blessed a student. Here's a portion of one from a middle school teacher:

> William was a student who was on his way to being retained in the seventh grade. In his case intelligence was not the problem, but rather a propensity for trouble. After being in the [TALKS] program and working with his mentor, William is now doing well enough to be promoted. Now, this is not to say that there haven't

been some bumps in the road, but connecting William to a positive role model has made the difference.[2]

For a guy whose heart is thrilled by helping children, that is a "feel good" report! But there's so much work to do. Will you consider joining the TALKS mentoring movement?

NOTES

1. Greg Kline, "Survey Says Area Needs Improved Youth Programs" (Champaign, Ill.) *News-Gazette* (April 18, 1999).
2. Private correspondence.

9

Mentoring Strategies for Turning Boys into Men

Harold D. Davis

—⚬⚬⚬—

Every boy needs a man in his face challenging him with wisdom regarding the critical issues and decisions in his life."

This statement drives the TALKS (Transferring A Little Knowledge Systematically) effort for mentoring young men. (For more information on the TALKS approach, please review chapter 8, "The TALKS Mentoring Curriculum and Approach.")

As a boy I was fortunate to have men in my life at various times who provided wisdom regarding life issues. I am a blessed man because of that. Through these men, God gave me so much that today my cup runs over. I believe that everything inside of my cup belongs to my family and me, and that everything that overflows my cup is supposed to splash onto those around me. That's the way it happened for me. I benefited from those who were willing to share their abundance with me. That's the way it must happen for boys today. Every concerned adult man must use his overflow to benefit the boys coming up behind him.

The psalmist speaks directly to our goal of equipping boys with testimonies of the goodness of God: "We have heard with our ears, O God, our fathers have told us, what work thou didst in their days, in the times of old. . . . In God we boast all the day long, and praise thy name forever" (Ps. 44:1, 8, KJV).

What a joy to have a son pray, recounting to God what he has learned of his heavenly Father from his earthly father. Fathers have a tremendous privilege, opportunity, and responsibility to share life experiences and the good works of God with their children. It has been my great personal joy to witness my son seeing the working of the Lord in his life and on his behalf.

But not every boy has the benefit of spiritual, fatherly instruction. The next generation of men is growing up in homes that have fallen apart or where parents are struggling. This is where a mentoring effort can effectively come alongside the family and provide needed support and guidance.

The TALKS mentoring approach provides a tested, satisfying way to connect men and boys. Here are the systematic steps that make it work:

- Assess the situation.
- Understand the levels of mentoring involvement.
- Take a personal inventory.

STEP 1. ASSESS THE SITUATION

The first strategy for turning boys into men is to assess the situation. That is, the mentor needs to ask, what's going on (where the boy is now) and what's about to happen (where the boy is headed). Proverbs 21:16 states, "The man that wandereth out of the way of understanding shall remain in the congregation of the dead" (KJV). Many youth today have veered from the narrow way of understanding onto the wide road that leads to destruction. If they continue in that direction it will land them in the congregation of the dead. There is a mass mentality at work among them. They are running in a pack, swarming together in the wrong direction like the stampeding swine in Luke 8:33: " . . . and the herd ran violently down a steep place into the lake, and were choked" (KJV).

Not one of the pigs stopped, looked around, or changed direction. While it is unwise to get in front of a herd of anything, it is possible to run alongside, grab one every now and then, and change that individual's course and direction. This is our objective as we commit ourselves to the task of turning boys into men through the TALKS mentoring effort.

STEP 2: UNDERSTAND THE LEVELS OF MENTORING INVOLVEMENT

After assessing the situation and understanding the need to get involved, a second strategy is to understand the various levels of involvement.

Mentoring exists on several levels. The entry level is considered "soft mentoring." Soft mentoring is basically structured companionship. The mentor also serves as a sounding board for the boy being mentored (the "mentee"). Soft mentoring includes academic tutoring and career and professional guidance.

The type of student involved in soft mentoring is basically a well-behaved kid who could benefit from additional adult companionship or guidance. This student is very impressionable and eager for assistance.

The adult who engages in soft mentoring must be caring and committed and must recognize the value to a young person of adult companionship. The mentor must be patient and consistent. Almost any mature adult can participate at the soft mentoring level.

A second level is "medium level mentoring." All of the requirements for soft mentoring are included at this level, along with the challenge to broaden the student's perspective and build self-esteem.

The type of student encountered at the medium mentoring level is still basically a good kid who may not have consistent or adequate adult companionship and guidance. This student may be functioning below his potential and may have given little or no thought to attending college or choosing a career. However, he is still very impressionable and open to assistance.

The mentor needs to be caring, committed, and willing to work with a youth through the normal adolescent life issues. The mentor needs patience and a sensitivity to youth culture and issues. Considerable thought must guide the mentor on appropriate attitudes and techniques.

The third level is "hard mentoring." At this level all of the previously stated skills are required, along with solid conflict resolution skills. The type of student at the "hard level" of mentoring is potentially a very good kid. He may come from a single-parent household with very little, if any, positive male or female guidance.

The mentor will need to use parenting skills in sharing knowledge on the responsibilities of manhood and womanhood. The mentor must be patient and willing to play several roles: teacher, coach, cheerleader, and resource person. The mentor will challenge the youth and will be willing to go where the youth "is," mentally, emotionally, and physically. Neighborhood and home visits are a part of the commitment at the hard level of mentoring.

The fourth and final level is the "hard-core" mentoring. The type of student requiring this in-depth mentoring is still reachable and impressionable but, having been exposed to a lot of negative influences, is desensitized. Such a student has had little or no positive adult influence and guidance. He is attracted to the seemingly easy way out and is looking for immediate gratification—quick money, instant pleasure. He is heavily influenced by his peer group and may have already become a part of the juvenile court system and may have been institutionalized.

Again, all of the previous skills are needed, along with a deeply serious commitment to mentoring. Hard-core mentoring is much like pastoral involvement. The mentor must be extremely caring, patient, committed, and willing to become basically a surrogate parent. He is willing to be in touch and on call. The mentor must understand the culture of young people, must be keenly aware of youth issues, and must be willing to remain an advocate for his mentee even while the young man continues to make poor decisions and mistakes. The mentor who engages in hard-core mentoring must emphasize the teaching of respect—for self, for others, for life, for authority, for the law.

STEP 3: TAKE A PERSONAL INVENTORY

The men who would mentor boys must make an honest, open, personal assessment of their own ability to serve effectively. Mentoring and discipling young people opens your life to the hand of God. When you mentor a young man, the Lord will also speak to you, and you must be open to God's cleansing and healing of your own personal problems. All of us have broken or missing parts. As we interact with young people, the Holy Spirit reminds us of areas where we need to mature. Psalm 139:23 (KJV) states, "Search me, O God, and know my heart; try me, and know my thoughts."

When one church where I shared the TALKS mentoring curriculum began the program, it wasn't long before the men serving as mentors decided to stop, back up, and deal with their own issues. I have found that the basic rule for mentors is that whenever God brings an issue up in you, it's time to deal with it.

Another area to consider is motive. Effective Christian service demands an understanding of one's motives. You need to know why you have decided to mentor. What inspired your decision? Was it evangelism? Was it a desire to fulfill the Great Commission? Was it a desire to be a positive influence in society? You must know why you are mentoring, or the inevitable rough spots will bring discouragement.

I am motivated to mentor because, as an adult Christian man empowered by the Holy Spirit, I understand the situation with today's young men, take my share of responsibility for it, and am willing to do something about it.

When taking a personal inventory, there are many things to consider, including:

• Cultural barriers. Are you comfortable in mentoring someone of a different culture?

• Your personality. Are you an extrovert or an introvert? A people-person or a loner? Will mentoring be easy for you, or will it be a stretch?

• Your personal schedule. How much time can you realistically commit to the effort?

• Financial issues. Will involvement in mentoring interfere with other commitments, such as work and family?

• Physical health. Do you have good health and stamina? You'll need both.

• Ministry gifts. Do your areas of giftedness correspond with the requirements for mentors?

• Personal deficits and deficiencies. Do you have significant unresolved emotional scars, insecurity, and instability that might trip you up?

Once you have thoroughly assessed the situation, have an understanding of the level of your involvement, and have honestly examined your ability for effective service, then you are ready to engage in mentoring.

FOUR MENTORING MODELS

There are four mentoring *models* that complement the four *levels* of mentoring that we discussed earlier.

The first mentoring model corresponds with the "soft mentoring" level. It is the *serendipitous model.* In this model you meet with the student and just hang out, such as for a walk through the park or the mall. And while you're doing this, credible and valuable things happen. This model has no particular structure or regularity. Many mentors serendipitously influence nieces, nephews, and other family members. Although it is low-key, such involvement can be very effective.

The next mentoring model, which corresponds with the "medium" mentoring level, involves *utilization of existing programs and organizations.* Why reinvent the wheel? One of the best-kept secrets in our country is the Boy Scouts of America. More churches today should seriously consider doing what many churches used to do: sponsor Boy Scout troops. Huge doors swing open for a child who can list "Eagle Scout" on his resume.

The third model is *tailor-made, special niche mentoring,* and it corresponds with the "hard" mentoring level. Mentoring occurs around a shared interest, something unique that two people come up with. Particular areas could be music, sports, or business.

The fourth model is *planned, didactic interaction.* It involves teaching, and it corresponds to the "hard-core" level of mentoring. The mentor and mentee get together for the sole purpose of teaching and learning. The interaction is based upon the fact that the mentor has knowledge that the mentee does not have. Boys, especially, need a man in their face challenging them.

BECOME A MENTOR OR MENTORING ADVOCATE!

I hope that you will select one of the models and actively participate in the mentoring effort. Remember how influential you are and how impressionable youth are.

Would you at least prayerfully consider mentoring boys? Thousands—millions—of the next generation of our nation's men need a little time and attention from a whole lot of men like you and me.

10

Older Women Mentoring Younger Women: Titus 2 in the Church Today

Susan Hunt

⸻

You must teach what is in accord with sound doctrine. . . . teach the older women to be reverent in the way they live, not to be slanderers or addicted to much wine, but to teach what is good. Then they can train the younger women to love their husbands and children, to be self-controlled and pure, to be busy at home, to be kind, and to be subject to their husbands, so that no one will malign the word of God.

—Titus 2:1, 3-5, NIV

This mandate is electrifying! Titus was pastoring a church on the island of Crete. The prevailing culture was pluralistic and decadent. Of all the things Paul could have told Titus to tell the women to do to combat that decadence, he bore down on the importance of older women encouraging and equipping younger women to live godly lives.

This was not a new concept. Throughout the Old Testament we are told that one generation is to tell the next generation the praiseworthy deeds of the Lord. In Titus 2, that characteristic of covenant life is simply made gender-specific. This fundamental quality of the culture of covenant life transcends time, geography, life-season, and life-circumstance.

Everywhere I go I meet young women who long for spiritual mothers. Some express a sense of loneliness, and yet they do not even realize that the disconnection they feel is because they do not have nurturing relationships with older women. Our postmodern age is characterized by isolation. The feminist movement made many promises, but the push for independence and autonomy has left women confused and alone. This is our opportunity. The time is ripe. Women are seeking answers. It is time for Christian women to step into this vacuum and show and tell the truth about womanhood.

But where are the older women?

In recent years I have observed a troubling phenomenon. Many women of my generation have relinquished this high calling of nurturing younger women. My generation has abandoned this calling for many reasons. Some simply do not know this biblical mandate. The church has not sounded this call for many decades. Some think they have nothing to offer. Some are intimidated by the intelligence and giftedness of younger women. Some have decided this is the season to indulge themselves. Some want to share their life experiences, but they feel isolated from the younger women and don't know how to bridge that gap.

I plead with the church to call and equip women for this ministry. God is gifting His church with incredible young women. They are a sacred trust. We must be good stewards of this gift. Many are first-generation Christians. Many are separated from their extended families because of the mobility of our society. We must exemplify the faith to them, and we must teach them how to show and tell the truths of biblical womanhood to the next generation. The implications of whether we accept or abandon this calling will reverberate for generations to come.

As we examine Paul's mandate to Timothy, your mind may be buzzing with questions: Am I an older woman or a younger woman? What do spiritual mothering relationships look like? How do I find them? Why should I make this kind of investment in the life of a younger woman?

We'll address those questions, but first we must step back and see the landscape on which spiritual mothering relationships are to be crafted and lived out.

THE COVENANT OF GRACE

God relates to us on the basis of a covenant of grace.

> *For you are a people holy to the LORD your God. The LORD your God has chosen you out of all the peoples on the face of the earth to be his people, his treasured possession. The LORD did not set his affection on you and choose you because you were more numerous than other peoples, for you were the fewest of all peoples. But it was because the LORD loved you and kept the oath he swore to your forefathers that he brought you out with a mighty hand and redeemed you from the land of slavery, from the power of Pharaoh king of Egypt. Know therefore that the LORD your God is God; he is the faithful God, keeping his covenant of love to a thousand generations of those who love him and keep his commands.*
>
> —DEUT. 7:6-9, NIV

Our relationship with the Lord is personal, but it is not individualistic. When He adopts us into His family, our relationship with Him means that we are also related to His other children. And our relationships with one another are to mirror our Father's relationship with us.

> *May the God who gives endurance and encouragement give you a spirit of unity among yourselves as you follow Christ Jesus, so that with one heart and mouth you may glorify the God and Father of our Lord Jesus Christ. Accept one another, then, just as Christ accepted you, in order to bring praise to God.*
>
> —ROM. 15:5-7, NIV

How does Christ accept us? Not on the basis of our performance, but on the basis of His grace. We do not earn our relationship with the Lord. It is all through sovereign grace from eternity past, when He set His affection upon us, to the moment in history when He gives us a new heart so we can repent and believe, to eternity future. God forgives us because Jesus paid our penalty, and He accepts us into His presence because we are covered with the righteousness of Christ. This is the covenant of grace.

We are to accept, love, and care for one another on the same term by which God accepts us—grace. The covenant way is not a way of isolation and independence.

When Cain killed his brother Abel, the Lord asked him, "'Where is your brother Abel?' 'I don't know,' he replied. 'Am I my brother's keeper?'" (Gen. 4:9, NIV). He was unaware that the answer to that question is yes. Living covenantally means that we are our brother's and sister's keeper. Women nurturing women is simply one way we live covenantally. It is as much a part of covenant life as gathering at the Lord's Table to remember His death until He comes again.

It is not optional. This gospel imperative is one way we express our Lord's command to love Him with all our heart, soul, and mind and to love our neighbor as we love ourselves (Matt. 22:37-39).

Unpacking the Passage

Now let's take a closer look at Titus 2.

To whom is this mandate given? It is interesting to note that this mandate is not written to women. It is written to the pastor of a church. It is a responsibility of church leadership to equip older women for this ministry. Women nurturing women is an essential element of healthy church life.

What is the foundation for this mandate? Titus 2 relationships are not to happen in a vacuum. They are to take place within the context of sound doctrine. As I explained in *Spiritual Mothering:*

> Paul's instruction to Titus to teach the women morality based on sound doctrine implies that the women were to be taught doctrine. . . . So these women were to be taught the principles of the Christian faith which would form the basis for their character. The soundness, or correctness, of the doctrine would give them a foundation from which to train the younger women.

Sound doctrine qualifies the kind of morality Paul is advocating in the command. Morality must be based on who God is and what He has done for us in Christ, or it will be purely subjective. Unless God is the reference point, there is no objective, absolute standard or authority for morality. If we begin anywhere else, our morality will degenerate to the level of the moral code of our environment. . . .[1]

What is the purpose of this mandate? The emphasis of the book of Titus is sound doctrine and godly living. God's glory is the overriding purpose of the relationships being discussed. This is not a self-enrichment program. These are covenant relationships that are centered on glorifying God by reflecting His grace to one another. In *Spiritual Mothering,* I give the following definition:

Spiritual Mothering: When a woman possessing faith and spiritual maturity enters into a nurturing relationship with a younger woman in order to encourage and equip her to live for God's glory.[2]

What kind of training is involved? The word translated "train" (Titus 2:4, NIV) is the Greek word *sophronizo.* It denotes "to cause to be of sound mind, to recall to one's senses. . . . The training would involve the cultivation of sound judgment and prudence. It suggests the exercise of that self-restraint that governs all passions and desires, enabling the believer to be conformed to the mind of Christ."[3] This is not just formal Bible instruction. This is teaching a way of life as we live in relationship with one another. It is passing on to younger women a biblical worldview that includes a biblical perspective of womanhood. It is helping them to think biblically and to apply biblical truth to all of life.

Who are the older women? This is not just about chronological age. It also involves life experiences and spiritual maturity. Every woman is both a younger and an older woman. There is someone who needs your life-perspective, and there is someone with a life-view that you need.

HOW DOES A WOMEN'S MINISTRY IMPLEMENT A TITUS 2 MINISTRY?

How do older and younger women find each other? The easiest way is when a church crafts a substantive women's ministry that teaches women God's truth about womanhood and helps facilitate covenant relationships that reflect our relationship with God.

The Titus 2 mandate is not a program—it is a lifestyle. However, it often takes some programming to jump-start spiritual mothering relationships. Here are a few suggestions to help a women's ministry leadership team encourage and equip women for a Titus 2 ministry.

General Observations

First, the women's leadership team needs to have a deep and long-term commitment to this scriptural mandate. It is not simply a matter of matching older women and younger women. This is a part of covenant life. Paul says that it is essential "so that no one will malign the word of God" (Titus 2:5, NIV).

Second, it is important for the leadership team to have their finger on the pulse of the women. Is spiritual mothering happening spontaneously and informally? If so, there may not be a need for a formal program. Perhaps the need is to simply celebrate what is happening by periodically asking women to share testimonies of how other women in the covenant community nurture them in the faith. Or if there are women who are on the fringe of church life or new believers who did not grow up in Christian homes, perhaps a spiritual mothering program is a way to enfold and nurture them.

Third, the Titus mandate was given to the pastor of the church. Paul instructed young Titus to equip older women in the congregation for this ministry. This equipping was to take place within the context of sound doctrine. It is a part of healthy church life. It is not just a *women's thing*. The commitment of church leadership is biblical and essential. If a decision is made to have a formal program, it is important to have the oversight and protection of the elders.

Consider this possible scenario: You announce that you are beginning a Titus 2 program, and you ask for volunteers to be spiritual mothers. A woman who has recently joined the church and appears to have great experience and maturity enthusiastically volunteers. You are unaware that she holds some theological positions and some views about women and marriage that are not consistent with Scripture. She is assigned to a young woman who, unknown to you, is having difficulties in her marriage because she resists the idea of headship and submission. Since such women who volunteer to be spiritual mothers have received no training, guidelines, accountability structure, or approved list of books to study, you have a disaster waiting to happen.

Fourth, careful and prayerful thought should be given to potential implications of a spiritual mothering program.

• How will spiritual mothers be selected?

• What accountability will spiritual mothers have and to whom?

• How can you avoid having young women disappointed because their spiritual mothers never cultivate the relationship?

• Who will monitor the program to see that it maintains its purpose and integrity?

• How will this program interface with the entire Christian education program of the church?

Fifth, even if it is decided to have a formal spiritual mothering program, women should be taught that this is to be a way of life and that the Lord will guide many women into nurturing relationships without the aid of a program. The legitimacy of these informal relationships should be highlighted and celebrated. The more a covenant community understands that this is part and parcel of community life, the less need there is for a formal program.

Sixth, spiritual mothering is not just a matter of chronological age. Even if all of the women in the church are the same age, there will be various levels of spiritual maturity and life experiences that equip them to nurture one another.

Seventh, the Titus 2 mandate is not limited to married women. Women should have a generational vision that includes singles, teens, and even little girls. Covenant daughters should be taught biblical womanhood by the women in the covenant community.

Eighth, if the elders and the women's leadership team determine that there is a need for a formal Titus 2 ministry, a subcommittee could be appointed to develop the purpose, procedures, policies, and plans. Simultaneously, enlist a prayer team to pray regularly for this committee. All plans should be submitted to the women's leadership team and then to the elders for approval. Elders may need to consider establishing policies for situations that will be referred to them.

Suggestions for a Titus 2 Ministry Planning Subcommittee

1. *Determine the purpose of the Titus 2 ministry.* For example: "The purpose of the women's ministry Titus 2 program is to help women establish covenant relationships with godly, older women who will encourage and equip them to live for God's glory."

2. *Develop a plan to enlist and train spiritual mothers.* This plan should clearly state the qualifications, how women will be recruited, how they will be approved by the elders, and how they will be accountable to the women's leadership team.

The training should be consistent with the doctrines and vision of the church. A "curriculum" should also include overarching principles of biblical womanhood.[4]

In some cases, a women's ministry may offer these studies through a Bible study program and then, growing out of that, identify women who are ready to be spiritual mothers. This long-term approach means that it will take several months for the training phase before moving to the next level of actually beginning the Titus 2 ministry.

Another option is to identify the spiritual mothers and then take them through the studies in a condensed format. They can read a book on their own, come together to discuss it, and then move to the next book. This could even be done in a training retreat.

This training should include a plan to train and enlist additional spiritual mothers in the future. Spiritual mothers should be trained to *reproduce* by encouraging their spiritual daughters to have the goal of becoming spiritual mothers themselves.

3. *Determine the target audience.* The number of spiritual mothers will determine the scope of the program. It is likely that the number of women desiring spiritual mothers will exceed the number of spiritual mothers. The purpose of the program should help determine

which women will have priority in being assigned spiritual mothers. For example, you may target women who are not able to attend regular women's ministry Bible studies and encourage those who do attend these studies to engage them in informal Titus 2 relationships.

When there are enough trained spiritual mothers, you may want to consider expanding the program to enfold teenage girls. Another long-term objective could be to provide a spiritual mother for every new female member of the church for three months.

4. *Develop guidelines that include things such as:*

• How spiritual mothers and daughters will be matched. This can be as simple as drawing names or as involved as finding common interests and experiences. Whatever method is used, the most important thing is to spend much time praying for the Lord to bring the women together according to His purposes for them.

• The duration of the formal relationship. Usually it is recommended that a spiritual mothering program run a year at a time.

• How to determine the shape of the relationship. Spiritual mothers should be encouraged to have good conversations with their spiritual daughters to ascertain needs, expectations, and realistic goals. Will they meet at a regular time or will it be more informal? Will they study and pray together or just meet for lunch and conversation?

• A list of approved books for spiritual mothers and daughters to read and discuss.

• How and where to refer problems that require pastoral or professional help. This should include cautions and clear parameters about dealing with crisis situations.

• How the program will be publicized. Publicity should be a tool to educate the entire congregation about the purpose of the program and to enlist prayer support.

5. *Outline a plan to maintain the vision and heart of the program.* For example:

• Have two or three gatherings a year for those involved in the program. This could include a sharing time, so the participants can learn from and encourage one another.

• Each year before women sign up for the program, promote it by having spiritual mothers/daughters give brief testimonies in church. Have a different testimony for each of three or four Sundays before the sign-up begins.

• At women's ministry special events, have women share testimonies about the blessings of Titus 2 relationships.

6. *Develop a plan to implement the program.* For example:

• There should be a Titus 2 coordinator or committee. Determine how this person/committee will be appointed, length of term, and how she or they will relate to the women's ministry leadership team.

• Women who complete the course of study will be asked to pray about becoming spiritual mothers. Those who are willing will fill out a form agreeing to the guidelines. These names will be submitted to the elders for approval. Those approved will be commissioned in a church service. They will commit to pray throughout the summer for the Lord to direct the committee in assigning them a spiritual daughter.

• The committee will determine how many spiritual daughters the program can accommodate, offer the program to the women, make assignments, and host a gathering for the spiritual mothers and daughters.

• At the end of the term, the committee will meet with spiritual mothers for evaluation, ask if they will serve again, and get their recommendations of spiritual daughters who completed all the studies and who may be ready to be spiritual mothers. In some instances a spiritual mother and daughter may want to continue for another year in order to complete the entire course of study. The committee will also determine if they need to provide another training time for women who may be interested in becoming spiritual mothers.

• Every opportunity will be used to keep the Titus 2 concept before the women at large through testimonies at special events, articles in newsletters, and public prayer for spiritual mothers.

THE GOAL

The goal of a Titus 2 ministry is not a dazzling, well-run ministry. Paul told the young preacher to equip older women with sound doctrine so they could train younger women "so that no one will malign the word of God" (v. 5, NIV). This is compelling. It is a gospel imperative. It is the way Christian women show and tell the next generation of women "the praiseworthy deeds of the LORD, his power, and the wonders he has done . . . so the next generation would know them, even the children yet to be born, and they in turn would tell their children. Then they would put their trust in God and would not forget his deeds but would keep his commands" (Ps. 78:4, 6-7, NIV).

And thus Christendom is advanced.

NOTES

1.   Susan Hunt, *Spiritual Mothering: The Titus 2 Model for Women Mentoring Women* (Wheaton, Ill.: Crossway, 1992), 39-40.
2.   Ibid., 12.
3.   W. E. Vine, *An Expository Dictionary of New Testament Words,* vol. 4 (Old Tappan, N.J.: Revell, 1940), 44.
4.   *Biblical Foundations for Womanhood* is a series of books designed to give women a biblical perspective on womanhood and thus to equip them for a Titus 2 ministry. For more information, call 1-800-283-2357.

11

TEACHING MANHOOD TO MEN

Robert Lewis

—∞∞—

Never—in nearly thirty years of pastoral ministry—have I experienced a more fruitful, productive, life-changing ministry with men in the local church!

It's a program we call Men's Fraternity, and it has revolutionized our church from top to bottom, and even moved us as a body toward greater influence in our community. We now have many men who believe they have what it takes and are equipped to accomplish significant ministry in their work, in their community, and even around the world.

Most gratifying to me, though, is the impact of Men's Fraternity on individuals. I have seen men come alive as they involve themselves in the lives of other men. Take Harry, an older gentleman in our church who had severe health problems. Once I went to see him in the hospital, and from his bed he told me that his health had declined after he had retired. "You know, I just don't have anything to live for," Harry said.

I thought, *Wow, Harry is in our church and he thinks he has nothing to live for? What's wrong with this picture?* Harry was an outstanding businessman and his marriage was strong.

"Harry, that's just not true; we can use you at church," I told him.

"Well, what can I do? I can't teach."

"Sure you can teach, Harry. You are a walking reservoir of unbelievable experiences that men would die to pick your brain on."

"I have failed a lot."

"That's the point! You have failed in some things, and from what you learned through those experiences you can tell young men what not to do, as well as what to do. What rich experiences you have to offer and stories to tell!"

Shortly after his hospital stay, Harry took me up on my offer. He became involved in Men's Fraternity. He was there the day, sometime later, when I challenged older men to reclaim the second half of their lives by investing down in younger men as mentors. I paused in that message and said, "All of you young men who would like a personal mentor, please stand up." About one hundred and fifty guys stood up. They didn't care who the mentor would be. They just wanted an older man to talk to.

So I turned to the older guys and urged them to take a risk and open themselves up to these younger men. Harry was one of those who made himself available.

About four years later, as I was at the athletic club working out at 6:00 A.M., Harry climbed on the treadmill next to mine. He looked healthy as a horse. "How's the mentoring going?" I asked him.

"Well," Harry said, "I have seven guys I am mentoring right now and I have five on a waiting list. Is that not incredible? Robert, it is the greatest thing I have ever done. I am reclaiming a whole season of my life as I pour myself into these guys. I still don't know anything, but these guys just want to talk. And being retired, I have plenty of time to talk. It has given me a whole new ministry, and those young men are just loving it."

That's just one story illustrating why I love the impact of Men's Fraternity. Before explaining how the program works, let me first offer some background on the needs of men and why a ministry like Men's Fraternity is so important.

THE NEEDS OF MEN

After many years of listening to men talk, as I worked toward an understanding of my own masculinity, I have listed what I believe are the common needs of most men.

First, *men need a safe place to go where they know someone understands them, where they don't feel alone.* If men feel welcome and understood, they will let their guard down and interact with other men over issues that may have been stuffed in their soul for years.

Second, *men need a compelling vision of biblical masculinity that they can grasp.* Men want to know what God intends for them. This vision will inspire and lift them during moments of challenge in the workplace and community, or when they are facing discouragement. The vision will recharge them. But it must be "user friendly"; the content must make sense in the context of their own lives.

Third, *men need time to effectively deal with issues relating to their manhood.* That is why a men's ministry should be more than a periodic rally. Seminars and rallies are excellent for motivating men, but they do not provide enough time for processing all the issues relating to their masculinity. Men are often cautious and do not move quickly toward a deeper perspective of who they are. Effective ministry must allow men to involve themselves with other men through ongoing interaction and rubbing shoulders with one another.

Fourth, *men need practical how-tos they can use and taste success with.* What they learn regarding things such as marriage, family, and career must connect with their day-to-day experience. Can they go out immediately and implement ideas at least at a rudimentary level? If the teaching does not work in real life, men will start ignoring what you tell them.

Fifth, *men need male cheerleaders.* These can be special peers or older mentors who come alongside to listen and offer encouragement. "You can do it!" said by an older man has a profound impact on a younger man.

Sixth, *men need a sacred moment where they know they have become not just a man but a biblical man.* Men need a reference point where they know they have crossed over into the promised land of responsible manhood and will stay there and grow. This need can be met through special ceremonies included in men's ministry.

Finally, *men need the church.* If the church and its pastors don't lead men to reclaim biblical manhood, most men will not pursue it with consistency, camaraderie, celebration, and courage.

THE MEN'S FRATERNITY DESIGN

I believe Men's Fraternity significantly meets all of these needs of Christian men. Let me tell you how the Men's Fraternity design looks now at Fellowship Bible Church in Little Rock. Believe me, this is not what we had at the start! We fumbled around and made many errors in many trials! But by God's grace we have made much progress.

Men's Fraternity runs twenty-six to twenty-eight weeks during the school year. We begin in early September and meet weekly until we break for the holidays—around December 10. We start again in mid-January and continue until the first week of May, when we have a "special graduation ceremony" completing the year and marking the accomplishments the men have made.

The preparation process begins early in August when we have a Men's Fraternity get-together for our leaders. We meet to plan and pray throughout the month, even going into the church auditorium, where Men's Fraternity will meet, and praying over every seat. This pattern of weekly prayer by the leadership team continues throughout the year.

Because Men's Fraternity is also an outreach opportunity, we run large ads in the newspaper about four weeks before Men's Fraternity begins. The ad lists topics and has photos of our host and myself. We also personally invite men from throughout the community. For example, one year all the salesmen from the local Merrill Lynch office came. One of the men belonged to our church, but the others came to hear subjects like "Becoming a Man," "A Man and His Life Journey," and "Twenty-five Ways to Love Your Wife." We encourage men to join Men's Fraternity in groups, because the more guys can get together with their friends, the quicker they will bond, open up, and share their lives with one another.

We are careful not to use Men's Fraternity as a recruiting device for Fellowship Bible Church. When our Men's Fraternity host welcomes men to the early sessions, he always says, "Guys, I just want to remind you that this Men's Fraternity is a community event, not a Fellowship Bible Church event. We are not here to recruit members for Fellowship Bible Church. If you are here from another church and something benefits you, take what has helped back to your pastor and encourage him to do something similar for the men of your church." And this has happened. Men's Fraternity-like groups have started in a Methodist and a Baptist church in our city.

We definitely welcome men from all churches and backgrounds. At one Men's Fraternity we had sixteen different churches represented. I remember once we asked everyone who didn't go to Fellowship Bible to stand, and 350 of the 700 men present stood up.

Men's Fraternity meets every Wednesday morning. Here's the schedule:

6:00–6:15 A.M. Coffee and fellowship
6:15–6:30 A.M. Host greets the men, gives announcements, prepares the way for the day's message
6:30–7:00 A.M. Message by pastor or the day's presenter
7:00–7:30 A.M. Small group interaction

Because Men's Fraternity is an outreach ministry, the first meetings have a more seeker, "non-churchy" feel. We want unchurched or marginally connected guys to feel welcome and safe. There will be many powerful "spiritual moments" in the weeks to come, but at the beginning we don't want to scare them away. Slowly the emphasis on prayer, Scripture, and Christian music increases. By about midyear, when we really hit Scripture hard, the men are comfortable and ready.

We end the year with each guy assessing all he has learned and putting together a "Manhood Plan" that lists goals for growth in his manhood in specific areas concerning his past, present, and future. The plan is first shared with his small group and then turned in to me.

The first week in May we have a sacred ceremony of graduation for every man who has completed his plan.

In the summer months many men continue to meet and interact in their small groups, usually around a breakfast. By that time, a number of them have formed some pretty intense friendships that will go on for life. Recently, I spoke to a physician whose group is still meeting five years after going through Men's Fraternity.

THE MEN'S FRATERNITY CURRICULUM

We have three years' worth of Men's Fraternity curriculum which, when we finish the cycle, we start over again. The first year is devoted to dealing with the issues of manhood. It also establishes a solid biblical definition of manhood that men can build their lives on. The second year deals with the two most important responsibilities in a man's life—his work and his woman. The final year speaks to a man and his life in the world, emphasizing personal gifting, his ministry in the world, and life as a great adventure.

Here is a more detailed explanation of the content of Men's Fraternity.

Year One

The first year, "The Quest for Authentic Manhood," is a primer divided into three sections. The first part deals with a "man and his baggage." Here we talk about the different wounds in a man's life and his misperceptions, misplaced expectations, hurts, and so on. This portion concludes with an explanation of depravity and the sinful nature that haunts us all. At our last meeting before the Christmas break, I share the gospel explicitly and urge unbelieving men to respond. At this point in the first semester, these guys now trust me enough to listen carefully, and a good number do stand up to indicate their desire to receive Jesus Christ. After the holiday break, we get into the Scripture more heavily and begin to build a theology of Christian manhood. The first year ends with the creation of a specific definition of "what is a man?"

Year Two

During the second year, the first semester covers "A Man and His Work" and the second semester "A Man and His Woman." In our church, we have some outstanding men like Doug Sherman, Dan Jarrell, and Dennis Rainey who have great expertise in these areas, so they present most of the weekly talks. Doug explores how a man deals with success, ambition, and serving Christ in the workplace. Dan and Dennis tackle the home and instruct men how to promote, protect, and honor their wives while investing wisely in their families.

Year Three

The final year of our curriculum is "A Man and His World." The first semester covers "A Man and His Great Adventure!" Here we teach what it means to walk with the Spirit of God while strategically considering how to live a life of real purpose and become a "difference maker" in the world. The second semester revolves around "A Man and His Design," which helps men understand their "gift mix" and what really motivates them. We help guys discern not only their gifts but how to employ them as a ministry in the world.

At the conclusion of the last year in Men's Fraternity, we challenge the men to determine what ministry they can now have with their gifts, how they can walk with God in a consistent way in the world, and how they intend to live with direction and purpose. We finish by asking the men to come back and bring other men the next fall and to become group leaders as the cycle begins again with Men's Fraternity One.

A First Morning at Men's Fraternity

Now that I've explained the design and content of Men's Fraternity, let me give you a brief tour to reveal what a guy coming for the first time experiences and feels on the opening day of Men's Fraternity.

The doors open at 5:45 A.M. If you drove up at this early hour, you would see that all the lights are on and music is playing when you enter the building. The mood is warm, bright, and cheerful. At the doors you are greeted by big smiles from men on the Men's Fraternity staff. Hot coffee is available at each of several "entry stations." The hosts at the doors and stations assume that on your first visit you are scared to death. You may not normally attend this church, or any church for that matter. So the host's job is to make you feel comfortable and safe. More than likely you will return to the same station each week and the hosts there will get to know your name and greet you more personally, laughing with you, patting you on the back.

As you enter, you will receive a sheet of paper that has the outline for the day's lesson and questions for your small group, which you'll find out about later. You will have until 6:15 A.M. to drink coffee and stand around and visit with other guys. The buzz grows through that early part of the morning.

Since outreach to seekers is a definite purpose of Men's Fraternity, the first ten to twelve sessions are as non-religious as possible. So the music you hear playing in the background is popular secular music; the leadership team has selected songs from the sixties to the present to fit the theme of today's message.

At 6:15, the entire group finds seats in the auditorium, and the host does the welcome and opening remarks for about ten minutes. At 6:25, he introduces me and I deliver the morning's talk. At 7:00, we break up into small groups. Since you are new and have no group, at our host's invitation you will meet in a group he will lead this morning. By the following week, you will be assigned to an existing group for the rest of the year.

You will grow to like your group. As time goes on and you recognize that this is a safe place, you will open up and begin sharing at a deepening level. If you have identified with the men and demonstrated transparency before them in dealing with your own manhood, by the third or fourth session your interactions in the groups will be surprisingly deep. I have had several counselors come to Men's Fraternity and observe that the level of transparency the group reached in two or three weeks is beyond what private counselors may reach in two or three months. Guys want to talk to guys. They just need someone to create the right environment and spark the conversation.

At 7:30, you will hear music begin to play, a signal that Men's Fraternity is over for the day. If you must, you are free to leave right then for work. Some men will hang around or go out to breakfast together. Tapes of that morning's message are provided at a resource table.

For a few of us, however, Men's Fraternity is not quite done at 7:30. Each week my host and I invite two of the small groups (fifteen to twenty guys) to join us for a simple breakfast. We only ask each group to do this one time during the whole year, and these times are scheduled far in advance. If a man can't do it at his scheduled time, he just can't. But most guys are able to meet with us.

Once breakfast is served, I'll say, "In the thirty minutes I have with you I want you to tell me what is working and what is not. What about Men's Fraternity is making a difference in your life? What is really helping you? What would you change about Men's Fraternity if you could?" This means on a weekly basis for the entire year I have a "focus group" telling me where I am succeeding and where I am not. It lets me know if I have overlooked some question. For example, someone might say, "You talk so much about your son. How would you do that with your daughter?"

When I hear that from enough guys, the next week I will incorporate the answer into my talk. This practice of debriefing keeps us from having blind spots in what we are teaching and in the general operation and effectiveness of Men's Fraternity.

STARTING A MEN'S FRATERNITY OF YOUR OWN

Is Men's Fraternity transferable to other churches? Most certainly yes, although I do urge some modification in most cases.

We are not trying to start Men's Fraternity "franchises" throughout America, but I estimate that about seventy pastors and thirty college ministries are now using this model. Since my passion is to influence men, I will gladly share the Men's Fraternity concept with anyone who thinks it might work in his church.[1]

If you are a pastor and ask me, "How can I use this?" here's my answer. I recommend that you *not* get a group of guys together and play the tapes. If your group or the church is very small and you have only a few men, that approach might work, and some have done it successfully that way. But in most situations I strongly suggest you yourself take the time and listen to the whole series (year one) from start to finish. There will be things you really like and things where you say, "I can do better than that." That's great! When you finish listening, then go back lesson-by-lesson and create your own personalized version. Remove whichever of my illustrations and other things you don't like, and put your personality and illustrations in. Call your men's ministry something different than Men's Fraternity if you like.

When you are done, you will have your whole first-year curriculum finished. Next, find your host (see below). After finishing your preparation, announce your men's ministry starting date and get ready to roll. If you are a layman or a staff member who does not have pastoral involvement or support, you can get a small group of guys together (probably not more than ten), listen to a cassette (by Fall 2002, we will have Men's Fraternity on video), hand out study sheets, and have your discussion. Men's Fraternity is adaptable to such an environment.

Here are two more tips to help make your Men's Fraternity a winner:

1. *Find the right host.* This is absolutely critical to the success of Men's Fraternity. He is not just a welcomer. He is a *host.* Here are some characteristics that are essential for this guy:

- He has to be well known in the community.
- He has to be well respected in the community.
- He has to be a good and warm communicator.
- He has to be creative and well organized.

God gave me that kind of man in Little Rock—Bill Smith. He answers all of these qualifications. Bill stands in front of the men and welcomes them, helps them get settled, and interacts with them. Since he knows the subject of my talk ahead of time, he will do things to get men ready for my presentation. For instance, if the topic is a man and his wife, Bill may have arranged to have a man come up and interact about his marriage. He can be quite inventive. One time during the first session in the fall, Bill was talking to the guys and pumping them up on what they would learn . . . when the house lights went off. On our screens we saw a three-minute clip from the Apollo 13 liftoff. The message was clear: "Today we're lifting off."

2. *Use technology.* If you have the ability to use technical aids in your talks, I encourage you to do so. Microsoft's PowerPoint is a good example. Men seem to respond well to different communication techniques that use computers, movie clips, and the like. Use these creatively, especially during the early sessions of Men's Fraternity.

Technical bells and whistles that are familiar to men can reduce the resistance of those not comfortable in church. In the early sessions I don't even open a Bible. I will say, "Just like the Scriptures say," and the Bible verse will come up on PowerPoint behind me.

Using media tools can really sink home a point. When I talk about roles in marriage, many men get uptight. I talk to them about marriage being a partnership between people, but if it is a true partnership, that may bring problems—since most business partnerships fail. I explain that you have to have someone to lead. This is how marriage works, I say. When I finish that particular talk I step off the stage, and as the lights go down, a video called "It Works," by the country music group Alabama appears on the screen. It takes the theology of marriage—what we are talking about that morning—and in a very emotional way, drives it home to the guys. The song tells the story of a young couple going to visit the husband's mom and dad. All through the time with his folks, the young man compares his "modern marriage" to the one he sees his mom and dad enjoying. The video shows powerfully that some aspects of marriage and male-female roles are never outdated. They are timeless and, yes, biblical. As the young couple drives off, the husband looks in his rearview mirror and sees his dad and mom hugging and loving one another. The last line of the song is, "It works." That powerful moment really gets the men thinking.

THE ONGOING MINISTRY OF MEN'S FRATERNITY

Some people are surprised to learn that we repeat the Men's Fraternity program every three years. I was a bit shocked myself with what happened at our church during the first repeat. When we came back to teach Men's Fraternity I again, I expected a whole new crop of guys. Instead many of the men who had gone through the first time were back, but they had recruited groups of friends, and the returning "vets" automatically became group leaders. At the end of the year I brought all those guys together and asked, "Why did you go through this a second time?"

They told me, "The first time we went through it we were kind of reacting emotionally and got excited about it. But the second time the material sank in at a much deeper level, and we also got to share the experience with our friends."

We now have done Men's Fraternity One four times, and I still have several hundred men who faithfully hear it again and again with their friends. Their joy is in seeing what it does with other men. My joy, however, has been in seeing the incredible changes in their lives.

Nothing I have done in my decades of ministry has had such far-reaching impact as this men's ministry. Nothing. Today hundreds of men serve as mentors with our children, students, and young adults. Hundreds more serve faithfully and willingly as small group leaders pastoring our large congregation up close. Others gather in weekly accountability groups because they have learned the value of cheering for one another as men. Others have courageously stepped forward in ministry ventures that our church would never have dreamed of doing without their creative leadership. The spiritual life and tenor of our whole church is deeper and higher today because we stumbled across the power that is unleashed when men discover their true masculine identity.

Most important of all is what I have observed in our men regarding their marriages and families. Hardly a week goes by that a wife in our church doesn't grab me and comment about the impact of Men's Fraternity on her husband.

Just recently, I was walking through a local mall in Little Rock when a young woman pulled me aside and said excitedly, "What did you do to my husband?" She then explained how her husband had been displaying spiritual initiative and direction he had never shown before. He was also involving himself in her life and in the life of their nine-year-old son with a passion that amazed her. "It's like he's a whole new man!"

As I walked away, I kept hearing those words, "He's a whole new man! . . . He's a whole new man!" And all because I, a pastor, had discovered a critically needed new ministry . . . teaching *manhood to men!*

NOTES

1. We have printed Men's Fraternity curriculum for all three years as well as tapes and videos of the messages. If you are interested in obtaining information or materials, go to the website www.fellowshipassociates.com, or call our Cross Reference Bookstore at 501-224-3238 for help.

IV

SECURING THE FAMILY'S FUTURE

———— ∞ ————

12

LEADING THROUGH
THE FOG

Steve Farrar

I know a heavy fog when I see one.

Where I grew up in Bakersfield, California, the schools never closed because of ice or snow, but every year they shut down because of fog. The murky air was so thick in the San Joaquin Valley that for as long as ten days you could not see the center line on the road or the house across the street.

I believe a moral fog as heavy as that has descended on our nation and, even worse, on the church of Jesus Christ. Everywhere Christians are confused and disoriented, and godly leaders are needed to lead us to safety.

What is responsible for the massive moral whiteout in our day? Can we reasonably predict what will happen next? I have three observations.

First, the foundations are being destroyed. The most important part of any structure is the foundation. Once a construction company was building a high-rise condominium, and on the day the foundation was poured, the ratios for the concrete were incorrect and there was more sand than cement in the mix. But since the concrete looked normal, no one noticed. Later the mistake was discovered, and it took almost two years and hundreds of thousands of dollars to fix that weakened foundation. A faulty foundation can cause a building, a family, a church, or a nation to collapse. David said, "If the foundations are destroyed, what can the righteous do?" (Ps. 11:3, NASB).

I believe America's freedoms and stable government, our prosperity and abundance, and many other blessings are the result of a solid foundation, much of it constructed by the Pilgrims. When those adventurous souls arrived on this shore, they didn't have much—the clothes on their back, some seed for crops, and a few tools. But they also had the most important raw material required to build a nation's "footers." They had the Bible.

A sightseeing trip in Washington, D. C., reveals the evidence of the raw material the Founding Fathers used to build the foundation: Scripture quotations are everywhere! But in our time that foundation of the Word of God is being destroyed.

But more sad to me is that the same erosion of the foundations is occurring within the church. An example of this is the debate over the proper roles of men and women. Today, many Christians won't even use the term "helper" for a wife, even though that's what God called her (Gen. 2:18), and even though it is a word He uses to describe Himself (Ps. 33:20). The wording of Genesis 2:18 is problematic for some in the church because they don't really accept all of Scripture as infallible truth—a sure sign that the foundation is being destroyed.

A second contributor to the moral fog is moral relativism. Allan Bloom wrote the insightful book *The Closing of the American Mind.* He was not a Christian but concluded that in essence America's greatness was a result of every home having a Bible, which represented the moral code of that family. Even if all family members were not devout, the Bible was considered an important source of moral values. Because "God said so" in the Bible, certain things were right and certain things were wrong. Thus every home stood on a foundation of moral absolutes.

But along came the 1960s and the ideology of moral relativism gained popularity. Moral relativism rejects the idea of a preeminent God and King who has the right to rule humanity as He chooses. With no absolute authority, absolute truth flies out the window. This opens the way for the lame sentiment, "That may be wrong for you, but that doesn't mean it is wrong for me." This, of course, is foolishness. Let me illustrate.

One spring I went to do a week's teaching at Biola University in Los Angeles, where our daughter Rachel was a student. I didn't arrive at my motel until about midnight, but I called Rachel and she said, "Dad, chapel is at 9:30. Why don't I come by and pick you up at 8:50?"

"That's great!" I said. I was exhausted and started to set the alarm clock in my room, but decided instead to ask the main desk for a wake-up call.

The next thing I knew I was awake and without a clue as to where I was. I groggily consulted my watch and saw 8:30. Then I remembered that I needed to be downstairs by 8:50! I jumped in the shower and thought, *Why didn't I get a wake-up call?* I hustled to get ready and went to the lobby. By 9:10 Rachel still hadn't arrived and I was getting upset because I had to be at Biola by 9:30. Finally I asked a guy, "Excuse me, what time do you have?" He looked at his watch and said, "It is 7:10."

Guess who had forgotten to reset his watch to Pacific Time! In the spirit of moral relativity I could have said, "No, no, it is 9:10." And he would have said, "No, it is 7:10." And I could have replied, "Well, maybe it is 7:10 to you but that doesn't mean it is 7:10 to me." That would have been ludicrous—like moral relativism is ludicrous.

Just as God has fixed time absolutely, so God has fixed morality absolutely. It can't be changed. There is no recall or referendum. Your general counsel can't change it. It *is* because *God* is.

Third, because of the increasing moral fog, we are a nation ripe for judgment. I have heard radio preachers say that judgment on our society is coming, but I wonder if "coming" is too optimistic? If you read Romans 1:18-32 and take an honest look at what is happening, are we perhaps already receiving judgment, or at least nearer to it than we ever dreamed?

There is a place on the Niagara River above Niagara Falls that is placid. But if you let your boat drift too far, the calm quickly turns to a raging current and you will go over the falls. You had better not cross that line. As a nation have we crossed such a line in regard to the judgment of God? The evidence is compelling: Moral chaos. Violence everywhere. The mocking of God. Filth in the media. Injustice. Schools and churches unsafe. If we are not being judged, we are overdue. Based on what we read about similar situations in the Bible, we know that when God finally responds, the answer is more disturbing than the silence. At some point He says, "Enough."

If God judged Israel, why would He not judge us? The sobering aspect for the Christian is that judgment begins with the household of God, and before it comes on the church, it comes on those of us who teach the Word of God to the church. James said, "Let not many of you become teachers, my brethren, knowing that as such we shall incur a stricter judgment" (3:1, NASB). I tremble for certain preachers and teachers. I know they love Christ, but they have caved in on important matters. I do not want to be arrogant or high-minded—I know how quickly I can cave in. We all have presumptuous sins and hidden faults. The Enemy is subtle. But we are the leaders and we must understand our challenge and wake up.

Breaking through the dark fog, though, is a shining light of hope: When judgment comes, there is a group of people God will bless, a remnant. The entire world can be crumbling down, but He will put His hand on those following Him with their whole heart. That is where I want to be. I challenge you to be there, too. I want to be one of the remnant. What will that require?

REBUILDING THE FOUNDATION

The church has a leadership crisis. We are desperate today for godly leaders. We need leaders with strong hearts who also have discernment, men like the sons of Issachar, who understand our time. It isn't 1955 anymore. It's not even 1990 anymore. If someone had walked up to you ten years ago and said "www.com," you would have thought, *Who let this guy out of the home?*

The leadership deficit is a huge problem in our churches. I once did some research and found 165 definitions of leadership. But the best one—no surprise—came from master communicator Howard Hendricks: "A leader is someone who leads." Don't miss the profound simplicity of that definition. Many people are confused about what leadership is. I find it helpful to distinguish between genuine leadership and synthetic leadership. First let me explain the impostor, synthetic leadership.

Synthetic leadership looks like the real thing, but it isn't. The phony leader is overly concerned with title, position, and perks. But those things don't make you a leader. You are only a leader if you lead.

At a luncheon a guy handed me the single most impressive business card I have ever seen. Top to bottom his card listed titles and positions. He was chairman; he was president; he was founder; he was chief executive officer; he was managing partner. Then on the flip side there was another list! As impressive as his card is, though, this man is only a leader if he *leads*.

Synthetic leadership makes a strong first impression and looks good. King Saul is a classic example of a synthetic leader. He had the great title of king. And he looked like a leader—a handsome man with chiseled facial features. If Saul were to enter a church sanctuary today we would all be attracted to him, because he stood head and shoulders above everyone else. The guy just looked great! But the problem with Saul was he didn't have the heart for leadership. Leadership is always an issue of the heart, because out of the heart comes such sturdy stuff as integrity and character.

Every time Saul's leadership was tested he failed miserably. Because his leadership was synthetic, Saul did not cut it and God finally said, "That's it. He's out of there." God found a new leader, a kid named David, who later would be described as a man "after God's own heart." David ended up on the run from Saul, because a synthetic leader is intimidated and threatened by an authentic leader. Genuine leaders lead out of the power of their lives—"You follow me as I follow Christ." That's it. They don't need a title or position.

The sons of Issachar understood the times and had a vision for what Israel should do (1 Chron. 12:32). Someone once asked Helen Keller if there was anything worse than being blind. She said, "Yes, having sight but no vision." Vision is critical for a leader.

I want us to be like the sons of Issachar about our times, because we are leaders in the church and the church is changing so quickly. Here are a few ideas on how to do this.

Get to the men. When I was a pastor in a local church, I always felt that the men were strategic. Joe Aldrich said a long time ago, "All of God's people are precious, but not all of God's people are equally strategic." He was absolutely right. It seemed to me then that if I could get to the men and influence them, about ninety percent of my counseling would be taken care of. If I could get the men in sync and help them understand what it means to be a man and the spiritual leader, I would be far down the road to having a healthy church.

Confront sin in the camp. God's judgment will consume us all if we don't come to grips with individual and corporate sin in the local church. Too often a scenario like this unwinds. Joe E. Evangelical teaches Sunday school, has been through Bible Study Fellowship, went to Promise Keepers and bought a hat, and is on the church board. This guy's spiritual resume is stellar, but then he hits midlife crisis and gets involved with a single gal in the choir. He leaves his wife and abandons his kids. What does the typical church do? *Nothing.* We back off. We punt. I am sick and tired of that!

What are you supposed to do when a brother is stuck in sin? You go and warn him. And if he doesn't listen to you, you go to a couple of other guys and say, "We know him and he is all messed up. We have to go talk to him about his sin and turn him back." This is not fun, but we do it because God commands it. If you don't think it is right to "judge" this way, check out 1 Corinthians 5:12, where Paul says we are to judge those who are in the church. We must implement the truth of Galatians 6:1 (NASB): "Brethren, even if a man is caught in any trespass, you who are spiritual, restore such a one in a spirit of gentleness; each one looking to yourself, lest you too be tempted."

"Defeminize" the church. I am not a woman-basher. What I will say next has much more to say about the state of the church's men than its women. We need to insist that Christian men be allowed their masculinity. Too many have the idea that it is unspiritual for a man to be aggressive. We have taken qualities like sensitivity, gentleness, and vulnerability and elevated them over aggressiveness, boldness, and

courage. Paul said, "Pray for me that I might have boldness." What men need to do is use the appropriate trait in the appropriate situation.

Could Jesus be gentle? You bet. The Lord is near to the broken-hearted, and He saves those who are crushed in spirit. We all have been crushed, and He has come right alongside and ministered gently to us. That is the appropriate, masculine quality to employ in that situation. But Jesus could be very tough, too, like the day He went into the temple and dumped over the tables. The bystanders didn't say, "Oh, what a nice, sweet guy." They said, "Let's get out of here!" The appropriate male qualities in that situation were aggressiveness, courage, and boldness.

Jesus loved us enough to get hurt for us. If Christ loved the church and gave Himself up for her, will not a Christian husband love his wife so much that he would get hurt for her, even die for her if necessary? We must be careful about creating and promoting a masculinity that is just nice and tender. Little boys are supposed to grow up to be men and, following in the footsteps of Christ, men are going to get hurt. But if we are programmed to fear getting hurt, our masculinity is damaged and diminished.

Seek personal holiness. My old professor Howard Hendricks often said, "If you worry about the depths of your ministry, God will take care of the breadth of your ministry." If we are willing to go deep with God, such things as church growth will fall into place. I am talking about the kind of people we will be. When God tests our integrity, truthfulness, and openness to Him, I want to pass those tests. For I know that ultimately He will bless me.

We are so messed up in the church because we have come to value giftedness over holiness. When some guy falls into immorality, our biggest question is, "How quick can we put him back in?"—because we worship giftedness more than the One who gave the gifts.

I am encouraged by the fact that none of us have to be gifted to tell the truth. What scares me more than anything is not telling the truth, not rightly dividing the Word of truth—saying, "This word means this," when it doesn't. We are going to stand before Him and be held accountable.

Those of us who are leaders, why don't we just love God, love His Word, and love the people in our care! We don't have to be a "Charles"—Spurgeon or Swindoll. We just have to stand up and tell the truth. God is looking for some guys who have the guts to put themselves on the line for Him and trust that He will take care of us. If we do that, we will lead others through the fog, and we won't have to be afraid or discouraged about the future. I want God to bless my life. His eyes "move to and fro throughout the earth that He may strongly support those whose heart is completely His" (2 Chron. 16:9). Let's be that kind of people to the glory of God.

13

Renewal in the Home

Crawford W. Loritts, Jr.

———⊗⊗⊗———

All roads lead back to somebody's house! The pivotal issues in life and ministry ultimately have to do with the health and wholeness of the family. I sometimes think that in our pursuit of insights that are tangible, transferable, and practical we forget this perspective.

What comes out of our homes should be the product of brokenness and utter dependence on God. One of my concerns these days is a pervasive tendency to think that the right system, the right insight, or the right "stuff" will produce spiritual change. Conferences, books, and manuals on our shelves are not the same thing as the move of the Spirit of God in our households.

God used a recent visit to my boyhood hometown to push the rewind button in my soul and remind me of my spiritual roots. I had not been back there in years. I was especially moved when I visited the small college nearby. I had only spent a year there but God did a deep, wonderful work in my heart.

As I pulled up to the campus and crossed over the bridge, I saw a sight that triggered a ton of memories. I spotted the little chapel where at the age of 17 I would go to pray at lunchtime and sometimes between classes.

Little did I realize then how those prayers would serve as the fuel for what God has done through these years in my life and ministry and family. I prayed that one day God would use me in a great way, that He would allow me to introduce many people to Christ. I prayed that

He would give me a godly wife. I prayed for children yet to be born. I asked God that they would give their lives to Christ at an early age, and that they would walk with God and be used by Him.

Several years later, while I was a student at Philadelphia Biblical University, I met Karen Williams and she became my wife. She is the joy of my life and the mother of our five children. She loves Jesus more than anything in this life. I am blessed beyond measure. I don't deserve her. God answered my prayer.

In the early years of my ministry with Campus Crusade for Christ, I traveled from one campus to another on speaking tours, and often Karen and the kids stayed home. Many an evening in a small motel in some little college town I would awake late at night, slip out of bed, fall on my knees and, often in tears, cry out to God, asking Him to not let my kids grow up bitter because I had to be away. I prayed that God would keep His hand on them and bless them. And God answered that prayer. Today our children are grown and are all walking with the Lord. Our oldest son is a pastor. Our youngest son left a promising baseball career and is preparing for the ministry. Both of our daughters (we have a daughter in heaven, too) are actively involved in ministering to others.

And so on that afternoon as I stared at that chapel, where as a seventeen-year-old I sought the face of God to provide for an unseen future, God flooded my soul with His grace and mercy. He reminded me that the blessing and favor we as a family have enjoyed and are experiencing are not because of our knowledge and expertise. It is precisely because I didn't (and still don't!) know what I was doing! But I did have an acute awareness that I needed Him—to provide a life partner for me, and to give me the wisdom and courage to know how to love her and to lead my family. In a word, anything of lasting value in my family is anchored in brokenness and produced by the Spirit of God.

Nothing but a family's surrender to the Lordship of Christ will transform it. You cannot program or demand revival in your home any more than you can program revival in your church. Sheer pragmatism will not produce spiritual results. But a family's life of brokenness and dependence on God will.

THE CONTEXT FOR RENEWAL IN THE HOME

How do we "prepare the way" for revitalizing life in the family?

First we must *make the commitment to see it happen.* In Joshua 24 the Israelites are called to gather in the Valley of Shechem to hear Joshua, their legendary leader, give his final address. In his talk he reminds the Israelites, the family of God, of their wonderful history and incredible heritage. He recounts the faithfulness of God and underlines the mark and signature of God's blessing, protection, and provision throughout their history and pilgrimage.

But as he looks into the faces before him, Joshua realizes that not everyone is as full of gratitude and appreciation for God's faithfulness as they should be. In fact some of them at best have "convenient" memories and at worst are obstinate and rebellious. He probably recognizes a few people who, no matter what he says, are going to do what *they* want to do. Against this backdrop Joshua boldly draws a line in the sand. He forces the people to make a choice, a decision:

> *Now, therefore, fear the LORD and serve Him in sincerity and truth; and put away the gods which your fathers served beyond the River and in Egypt, and serve the LORD. And if it is disagreeable in your sight to serve the LORD, choose for yourselves today whom you will serve: whether the gods which your fathers served which were beyond the River, or the gods of the Amorites in whose land you are living; but as for me and my house, we will serve the LORD.*
>
> —JOSH. 24:14-15, NASB

Joshua wants this family of God to decide where their loyalty and devotion will be. Make up your mind! What are you going to do? Whom are you going to serve? To whom will you give your ultimate allegiance? Even this great warrior of God realizes that he cannot make up their minds for them. As their leader he has done what God has told him to do. He has instructed them. He has relayed God's expectations and directives, but he knows that now they must make the choice.

Every parent needs a similar perspective. We cannot make our children walk faithfully with the Lord. There has been much erroneous teaching in Christian circles on child-rearing that makes assumptions about things that God never promised. Controlling our children and their environment, exposing them to the truth of God's Word, and editing the "input" into their lives cannot guarantee that they will become vibrant, obedient followers of Christ. The "life or death" issue has to do with their choosing, making a decision about what they have seen, heard, and been exposed to.

Our families need to know that God's faithfulness—what He has invested in us—demands a decision from us. His history in our lives is not just the stuff of warm memories and cherished food for thought meant merely to be fondly discussed and shared at family gatherings. It ought to call us to commitment, to make the kind of life choices and decisions that demonstrate the depths of our gratitude and deep appreciation for God's unfailing mercy, grace, and faithfulness in our lives. We need to call our families to undivided commitment and loyalty to the God of the ages!

Our homes today need to be what we want homes in future generations to be. Perhaps that's what Joshua had in mind when he said, "As for me and my house, we will serve the Lord." This carries the distinct ring of holy resolve. Joshua is reaching back and grabbing onto God's faithfulness and is also pointing to the only thing that will give value and meaning to the future: serving the Lord. It is for this reason that he forces a decision.

Cultural Christianity has anesthetized us. We don't see or appreciate the need to make this kind of life-altering decision. The word *serve* suggests a single focus. It points to who and what will capture our passion and determine the direction of our lives. It's as if Joshua was saying that serving God is not just a part of what our family does, it is who our family is.

This perspective carries with it a sense of accountability and the necessity of the parental modeling of what we want our children to build their lives on. Our families need to be the visible representation of the power of God at work in our lives.

Parents set the tone and the direction of the home. As our children watch us they must not see hypocrisy and inconsistency. Neither should they be the victims of heartless legalism, which is based on rules and regulations devoid of personal relationship and the love and grace of God. *In short, parents must be models of the renewal and revival they desire for their children and for future generations.*

GOD'S REQUIREMENTS FOR RENEWAL

It seems as if every Christian leader who wants to bring America to its knees will quote 2 Chronicles 7:14. But the injunctions in this verse are specifically addressed to those who have a relationship with God and not to unbelievers. These words speak to the moral and spiritual integrity of God's people in the context of a broken and fallen world desperately in need of deliverance and hope. These words were not given as leverage for Christians to "beat up" on an unrighteous society, but as a prescription for God's people to experience renewal.

The words uttered by God in this pivotal verse are in the context of the dedication of Solomon's temple. The focus of the dedication ceremony is fervent prayer, pleading for God's blessing on the temple and on His people. God then appears to Solomon in the evening and assures him that He has heard his prayers and that He has chosen the temple as a place of sacrifice and a place where He will dwell (2 Chron. 7:11-12). But God knows that His people will not always remain faithful to Him, and that He will have to occasionally get their attention by sending judgment. So He says in verse 13, "if I shut up the heavens so that there is no rain, or if I command the locusts to devour the land, or if I send pestilence among My people . . ." In other words, there may be times when our lives and homes are unraveling so much that we will need to follow the prescription that He has outlined in verse 14:

> *[If] My people who are called by My name humble themselves and pray and seek My face and turn from their wicked ways, then I will hear from heaven, will forgive their sin and will heal their land.*

Again, the target of these words of correction and renewal is God's people. It is as if God says, "I am talking to you and not to the foreigners who are living in the country."

During the last ten years we Christians have been griping about almost everything—the school system, politicians, atheists and naturalists, humanists and philosophical relativists, the ACLU, drugs, crime, and on and on. Of course we need to speak out against sin, but it seems to me that our posture is more often than not one of self-righteousness and not self-examination. The world is sinning because it is acting consistent with its nature. Complaining to the world about what it is doing is, in the words of Chuck Colson, like getting angry at a blind man for stepping on your foot. The real problem is that too many of us in the church, the family of God, are in sin. Ray Ortlund, Jr., rightly observes, "Perhaps we don't see more repentance in the world because the world doesn't see much repentance in the church."

This perspective applies to our Christian homes as well. As we live the Christian life, we should try to turn our families into what we would like to see society become. Our posture toward the world and toward the issues of our times ought to be that of a credible Christlike witness and not a finger-pointing condemnation. We ought to teach our children to "contend for the faith" and to hate sin in all of its forms and to boldly live righteousness. And as parents, if we really want to raise godly children, we must never forget to take personal responsibility for our own holiness. As the old spiritual says, "It's not my mother, not my father, but it's me, O Lord, standing in the need of prayer."

After God clearly identifies the audience (His people), He outlines four requirements that we must meet in order for there to be renewal and blessing in the "land."

The first requirement is that we must "humble" ourselves. The humility spoken of here is what our response *ought* to be when there is the signature of God's judgment around us. It is a brokenness born in our hearts because of the sin and its devastation. This is a heart that not only responds to but also identifies with that same propensity and ability to be swept away with the sins so evident in our society. It acknowledges the pain and agony that sin brings to the heart of God. It says, "Whatever they are doing I either have done or I am capable of doing!"

It is the cry of helplessness and dependence on God for His help and deliverance.

I am all in favor of teaching and encouraging our children to develop appropriate confidence and self-reliance, but we must be careful not to go too far and somehow push them toward smugness and arrogance. I think that's exactly what we do when we underscore the sins of those around us and declare how bad "they" are without connecting with the sinful inclination to "wander" that is in all of us.

We isolate ourselves. We erect our Plexiglas walls of protection and separation from "those" unbelievers and then toss our "gospel" grenades of criticism and denunciation over the walls at them, all the while leveraging the grace of God to feed a sense of self-righteousness. A humble heart, however, first acknowledges its own life of sin.

The second requirement is to "pray." God's power is released through the believing prayers of His people. When we are in the midst of judgment, that is not the time to "roll out our strategy" and hurl accusations at the "sinners in our land." It is a time for earnest prayer.

Let me ask a few questions. Are you and your family praying for our country? Are you praying for non-Christians to come to the Savior? Have you gotten so angry and disgusted with the ways of the "unrighteous" that you have forgotten that the only way they are going to change is if God changes them?

One reason why there is no compelling sense of mission in some of our Christian homes, I believe, is because our prayers are self-serving. Think about it. When we spend so much time praying about "our needs" and so little time praying for lost people, are we not being far too concerned about ourselves? If we prayed for unbelievers and for the conditions of our land, then, I believe God would give us His heart for lost people and show us how to reach them. It begins by dropping to our knees on their behalf.

The third requirement is to "seek My face." This is an interesting expression. It implies a passionate, "prioritized" search for God, to find out what He is up to. In other words, whenever we sense danger, we should drop everything and look for God.

I will never forget the time I was in a department store looking for ties. Our youngest son, Bryndan, who was about eighteen months old, was with me. Bryndan was holding on to my pant leg as I examined the ties, and as long as I felt the tug of his little hand I knew where he was and everything was okay. But I got really into looking at these ties and forgot about Bryndan. Then it dawned on me that I no longer felt the tug on my pant leg. My son was gone, and my reason for being in that store instantly changed. Ties were suddenly unimportant, as well as everything else in the store. I was consumed with finding my son. A few frantic moments later I found Bryndan hiding behind a rack of clothes. Of course he thought it was great that Dad had to come find him, but I didn't think it was too funny!

The judgment of God is meant to rock our private worlds. It is meant to cause us to examine our priorities and passions. It is a mirror to show us how things really are and not what we think they are. It's as if God takes a step back and says, "If you want me, then walk out of your self-absorption and complacency and make me the sole object of your desire!" Simply said, the judgment of God is meant to get us to seek Him.

Oh, how our families need to be consumed with a longing for God! Who God is and what He wants are ultimately the only things that matter in life. Our families need to interpret their sin and the sinfulness of our culture as God's call to get busy seeking God. God Himself is our only solution.

The fourth requirement is repentance, to "turn from [our] wicked ways." God desires His church to reflect His character in the world. When we embrace the values and sinful lifestyles of our culture, He is not pleased. We need to look closely at our lives and listen to the voice of God and determine what we need to repent of, and then repent.

Although it can be quite difficult, repentance is our friend, our ally. It should be embraced as a lifestyle, an identity. The Puritans referred to themselves as "Repenters." I like that, because it aptly points to repentance as the path, the means of experiencing God's forgiveness, of becoming Christ-like, and of demonstrating authentic Christianity.

We need to encourage each other, in our homes, to embrace this perspective on repentance. The home should be a place where this kind of authentic Christianity is nurtured and developed. It should be a place where, when we sin and fail, we understand that there is repentance and forgiveness. Then we will be able to walk out of our homes into a waiting, watching world with a clean heart. Then we will be not "sniping at issues," but bringing hope to the world in the name of Jesus Christ because we have first done business with God.

THE BLESSINGS OF RENEWAL

God says to Solomon that when these four requirements are met, then He promises to do three amazing things:

God hears us. "Then I will hear from heaven" is something of a double entendre. Literally, God hears our cry because we have met His requirements; we have done what He has instructed us to do. But also, when we do what God tells us to do, then we have the focused attention of heaven. Think of it. All of heaven's resources are available to us when we obey God!

I remember when our oldest daughter, Heather, was about two-and-a-half years old. I was sitting in my favorite chair one day reading the paper, and Heather was talking to me but I wasn't giving her my attention. She then jumped up on my lap, knocked the paper out of my hands, grabbed my face with her two little hands, looked me square in the eyes, and said, "Daddy, I talkin' to you!" You see, Heather didn't just want my ears; she wanted my total attention. Our surrender and complete obedience to God grabs God's heart and lines us up for His favor and heaven's resources.

We experience His forgiveness. Look at these sweet words: "will forgive their sin." God does not want His children to wallow in guilt. He has made provision for their sin. Our problem is that we so often want His blessing and favor without repentance. But there is no experiential forgiveness without repentance. It is when we come to the end of ourselves and acknowledge our sin and failure before Him that He rushes to us and wraps His loving arms around us and whispers in our ear that sweet word, "Forgiven."

The sequence is important here. Before anything is said about the land being healed, God speaks a word of healing for the heart. Before there can be blessing in the environment, God has to do a work in the individual heart. The culture and society is not a problem or a challenge to God. Once God gets His people cleaned up in their hearts, then look out, world!

Our homes need to celebrate our forgiveness. Our family members need to know that God's primary prerequisite for usefulness and blessing is forgiveness. He uses us not because we are perfect, or talented, or connected. He uses us not because we have never failed. No, He uses us because we have brought our sin and failure to Him and He has said, "Forgiven."

He blesses our environment. God says that He will "heal their land." God will remove His judgment from their environment because they have been obedient to Him. Isn't it interesting that God does not say that He will heal *them,* but that He will heal their land? Our vibrant, renewed life will "spill over" into our environment. In other words, God will bless those who come in contact with us because we are being obedient. When He showers us with blessing and favor, they get wet, too. I really believe that businesses and government administrations and other enterprises are successful to a large degree because of the presence of godly believers. God blesses what such believers are associated with because they have met His requirements.

Our families need to know that our walk with God is everything! We need to teach and model before them that God Himself is the source of all that we are and all that we will ever need. There is never any need to compromise our walk with God or our spiritual integrity. May God grant us the holy resolve of Joshua, that we may say with him, "As for me and my house we will serve the Lord."

APPENDIX:
THE DANVERS STATEMENT

The "Danvers Statement" summarizes the need for the Council on Biblical Manhood and Womanhood (CBMW) and serves as an overview of our core beliefs. This statement was prepared by several evangelical leaders at a CBMW meeting in Danvers, Massachusetts, in December of 1987. It was first published in final form by the CBMW in Wheaton, Illinois, in November of 1988.

RATIONALE

We have been moved in our purpose by the following contemporary developments which we observe with deep concern:

1. The widespread uncertainty and confusion in our culture regarding the complementary differences between masculinity and femininity;

2. the tragic effects of this confusion in unraveling the fabric of marriage woven by God out of the beautiful and diverse strands of manhood and womanhood;

3. the increasing promotion given to feminist egalitarianism with accompanying distortions or neglect of the glad harmony portrayed in Scripture between the loving, humble leadership of redeemed husbands and the intelligent, willing support of that leadership by redeemed wives;

4. the widespread ambivalence regarding the values of mother-

hood, vocational homemaking, and the many ministries historically performed by women;

5. the growing claims of legitimacy for sexual relationships which have Biblically and historically been considered illicit or perverse, and the increase in pornographic portrayal of human sexuality;

6. the upsurge of physical and emotional abuse in the family;

7. the emergence of roles for men and women in church leadership that do not conform to Biblical teaching but backfire in the crippling of Biblically faithful witness;

8. the increasing prevalence and acceptance of hermeneutical oddities devised to reinterpret apparently plain meanings of Biblical texts;

9. the consequent threat to Biblical authority as the clarity of Scripture is jeopardized and the accessibility of its meaning to ordinary people is withdrawn into the restricted realm of technical ingenuity;

10. and behind all this the apparent accommodation of some within the church to the spirit of the age at the expense of winsome, radical Biblical authenticity which in the power of the Holy Spirit may reform rather than reflect our ailing culture.

PURPOSES

Recognizing our own abiding sinfulness and fallibility, and acknowledging the genuine evangelical standing of many who do not agree with all of our convictions, nevertheless, moved by the preceding observations and by the hope that the noble Biblical vision of sexual complementarity may yet win the mind and heart of Christ's church, we engage to pursue the following purposes:

1. To study and set forth the Biblical view of the relationship between men and women, especially in the home and in the church.

2. To promote the publication of scholarly and popular materials representing this view.

3. To encourage the confidence of lay people to study and under-

stand for themselves the teaching of Scripture, especially on the issue of relationships between men and women.

4. To encourage the considered and sensitive application of this Biblical view in the appropriate spheres of life.

5. And thereby

• to bring healing to persons and relationships injured by an inadequate grasp of God's will concerning manhood and womanhood,

• to help both men and women realize their full ministry potential through a true understanding and practice of their God-given roles,

• and to promote the spread of the gospel among all peoples by fostering a Biblical wholeness in relationships that will attract a fractured world.

AFFIRMATIONS

Based on our understanding of Biblical teachings, we affirm the following:

1. Both Adam and Eve were created in God's image, equal before God as persons and distinct in their manhood and womanhood.

2. Distinctions in masculine and feminine roles are ordained by God as part of the created order, and should find an echo in every human heart.

3. Adam's headship in marriage was established by God before the Fall, and was not a result of sin.

4. The Fall introduced distortions into the relationships between men and women.

• In the home, the husband's loving, humble headship tends to be replaced by domination or passivity; the wife's intelligent, willing submission tends to be replaced by usurpation or servility.

• In the church, sin inclines men toward a worldly love of power or an abdication of spiritual responsibility, and inclines women to resist limitations on their roles or to neglect the use of their gifts in appropriate ministries.

5. The Old Testament, as well as the New Testament, manifests the equally high value and dignity which God attached to the roles of

both men and women. Both Old and New Testaments also affirm the principle of male headship in the family and in the covenant community.

6. Redemption in Christ aims at removing the distortions introduced by the curse.

• In the family, husbands should forsake harsh or selfish leadership and grow in love and care for their wives; wives should forsake resistance to their husbands' authority and grow in willing, joyful submission to their husbands' leadership.

• In the church, redemption in Christ gives men and women an equal share in the blessings of salvation; nevertheless, some governing and teaching roles within the church are restricted to men.

7. In all of life Christ is the supreme authority and guide for men and women, so that no earthly submission—domestic, religious, or civil—ever implies a mandate to follow a human authority into sin.

8. In both men and women a heartfelt sense of call to ministry should never be used to set aside Biblical criteria for particular ministries. Rather, Biblical teaching should remain the authority for testing our subjective discernment of God's will.

9. With half the world's population outside the reach of indigenous evangelism; with countless other lost people in those societies that have heard the gospel; with the stresses and miseries of sickness, malnutrition, homelessness, illiteracy, ignorance, aging, addiction, crime, incarceration, neuroses, and loneliness, no man or woman who feels a passion from God to make His grace known in word and deed need ever live without a fulfilling ministry for the glory of Christ and the good of this fallen world.

10. We are convinced that a denial or neglect of these principles will lead to increasingly destructive consequences in our families, our churches, and the culture at large.

We grant permission and encourage interested persons to use, reproduce, and distribute the Danvers Statement. Visit the CBMW webstore (www.cbmw.org) or contact us (888-560-8210) to place an order.

General Index

SCRIPTURE INDEX